THE COACH'S ART

THE COACH'S ART

BY
JACK RAMSAY
WITH
JOHN STRAWN

TIMBER PRESS
FOREST GROVE, OREGON

THE COACH'S ART
JACK RAMSAY WITH JOHN STRAWN

©Copyright 1978 by Jack Ramsay

All rights reserved.

Library of Congress Cataloging in Publication Data

Ramsay, Jack, 1925-
　The coach's art.

　1. Ramsay, Jack, 1925-　　2. Basketball coaches—United States—Biography.　I. Strawn, John, joint author.　II. Title
GV884.R33A33　　796.32'3'0924[B]　　78-5458
ISBN 0-917304-36-5

PRINTED IN THE UNITED STATES OF AMERICA

Cover and book design by Charles S. Politz/Design Council, Inc.

Timber Press
P.O. Box 92
Forest Grove, Oregon 97116

DEDICATION

*To every player who has played for me
at the high school, college and professional
levels—know that each of you is remembered
and that your collective image is etched
upon the pages of this book.
Jack Ramsay*

TABLE OF CONTENTS

PART I   GETTING READY

    1. COMING TO PORTLAND   3
    2. LEARNING THE GAME   17

PART II   THE COACH'S ART

    3. THE TEAM GAME   37
    4. RAMSAY BASKETBALL   69
    5. PLAYING IN THE NBA   133

PART III   THAT CHAMPIONSHIP SEASON

    6. BUILDING THE BLAZERS   153
    7. WINNING THE CHAMPIONSHIP   167

INTRODUCTION AND ACKNOWLEDGEMENTS

I have thought about what coaching is for most of my working life. I believe I now know many of the elements essential to doing it well. It troubles me that popular misconceptions about what a coach does inhibit many of basketball's growing number of followers from fully appreciating the game. I'd like to help remedy that. Spectators watch games, after all, but few understand what makes it possible for a team to play well. A great team playing within itself, playing with control and purpose, is beautiful to watch. Good play seems almost effortless. Five separate wills blended into a single whole, playing with one purpose—to win, yes, but by playing its own game, a game in which it believes. Behind the seeming ease with which a great team plays lie hours of preparation. I want to take you behind the scenes, to look at what leads up to the game itself.

I love the game of basketball and want to see it played as well as it can be played. That can't be done unless a *team,* led by a coach, has a clear idea of what it can do and how to accomplish what it intends. Teams have personalities, but they are not casually acquired. A successful coach, whatever style of play he coaches, gives his team its character. Coaches are the authors of what happens in a game.

The Coach's Art is not, however, an Xs and Os book, not a technical treatise on basketball strategy or the rules governing play. It is, rather, an essay on coaching as a complex human art. A coach develops ideas, communicates them to his players, and through them tries to realize his conception of how the game ought to be played. Just how that gets done— and how I learned to do it—is the subject I want to examine. My own coaching career has taken me through every level of play, from high school to the NBA. I want to review that journey. At every stage, I have learned about the game. The players in the NBA are the best in the world, but the ingredients for successful team play in the NBA are the same as anywhere else. A coach's ideas are judged everywhere by a single rigorous criterion: Do they produce winning teams?

In 1977, the Portland Trail Blazers won the NBA World Championship. In doing so, they played the game the way I had always hoped to see it played. It was a very satisfying experience, and one I want to share. I hope everyone who reads this book, whether player, coach or fan, will enjoy learning something about what I do as much as I enjoy doing it.

I want to recognize with sincere appreciation the skilled craftsmanship, wisdom and diligence of John Strawn, who put into meaningful order a mass of material and whose proddings for anecdotal illustrations have, I hope, breathed a more vibrant life into this work.

I also acknowledge the work of Sandy Sedillo for transcribing miles of cassette tape which had on them the distracting background noise of airplane engines, traffic sounds, phone and doorbell ringings, and dogs barking—not all of which, fortunately for her, occurred at the same time.

I want to thank Bill Zavin for his clear and precise illustrations of the basketball theory depicted here.

I am especially indebted to my Blazers for the execution of my game with the precision necessary for this story to be told; and I thank them for being the kind of people who have made their story a pleasure to tell.

And, lastly, I appreciate the presence of "the Blazer road gang" of Jack McKinney, Ron Culp and Bill Schonely; their easy companionship reduced our long NBA road trips to quick sprints through the country.

PART I: GETTING READY

COMING TO PORTLAND

CHAPTER I

"THERE'S one more thing, coach."

"What's that?" I asked Bill Walton as he shifted uncomfortably in his seat, trying to ease the pressure on his cast-encased left arm.

"Don't," he advised, "assume that we know anything."

Nothing Bill said could have pleased me more. Every coach likes to hear his players acknowledge their need to improve, but I can't think of another player in the NBA who would have said what Bill did. He thought that all the Blazers, himself included, needed fundamental drilling in the basics of good basketball. I thought it was remarkable that one of the most gifted players in basketball would tell me that he and his teammates would benefit from working on the most elementary aspects of the game. It was a good omen, a portent of the pleasures which lay ahead.

I was elated as I left Bill's home. My mind was racing ahead to plan the practice sessions and drill work my new team would require. Just the day before I had been named as the coach of the Portland Trail Blazers, the fifth in the club's six year history. The meeting with Walton, the young center whose promise had been eclipsed by injuries during his first two NBA seasons, was my first official order of business. He was the principal component of the team I wanted to assemble. His ability to defend, rebound and pass was crucial to the success of the game I wanted to play. I had sketched for Bill an outline of the running game I planned to use, describing the basic offensive pattern we would employ. I told him we would use the turnout, the basic crossing under action of the wingmen on the fastbreak. Bill gave me a quizzical look. "A turnout? What's a turnout?" A turnout, I told him, is a move by one wingman across the lane to set a screen for the wingman on the opposite side of the floor on a three-on-three fastbreak. Bill's casual nod indicated his understanding of what I had described. A year later, after observing a session at the Blazers' tryout camp for new players, Bill shared with me his opinion of the prospects. "I can't believe these guys don't know what a fucking turnout is." I couldn't help but smile in recollection of our first meeting.

Bill Walton was the hub of the team I wanted to assemble.

Bill understood well and liked his projected role in the game plan I summarized for him. I told him the kind of players we would need—quick guards, a quick small forward, a rebounding big forward and, of course, a center who could play the way Bill does. We didn't have all of these players yet, but I thought we could get them. Bill agreed. We were both confident that the Blazers could become a winner. The cast Bill wore had been put on earlier that summer after a screw was surgically inserted in his wrist to aid in healing a broken bone. He assured me that he would start to work on the conditioning that our running game required as soon as the cast was removed. By the middle of August Bill was running eight miles a day.

Bill was not the only player with whom I met in those early days as the Blazers' new coach. I thought of Bill as a first among equals, just as his teammates did later in electing him team captain. It is teams which win basketball games, however, and there were twelve key players on the Blazers' first championship team. During my first two weeks on the job, I talked with most of the players. Why, I asked each of them, did he think the team hadn't won? What did he think had to be done to make the team a winner? I wanted to learn more about each player, too; I was interested in meeting the people he lived with, in discovering his other interests and the kinds of things he valued. The conversations I had were instructive.

The responses to the questions I asked were varied, indicating to me that the team lacked a clear sense of what it had to do. Several players thought that the injuries the team had suffered—and particularly the injuries to Walton—had kept the team from winning. One thought the team just hadn't played well together, an opinion shared by another player who noticed too much bickering on the team. Yet another thought that Lenny Wilkens, their former coach, had not demanded enough of them. Despite the problems these answers pointed to, however, there was a consensus among the players that the team had the potential to win.

I previewed for the other players, as I had for Walton, the roles I saw them performing in the game I wanted to play. I told them what they could expect in our fall training camp, describing the routines we would follow in our practice sessions. Perhaps most importantly, I gave each player my frank evaluation of his play as I had seen it from the opposing coach's bench. I wanted to offer advice on how I thought he might improve, but I was equally interested in observing his reaction to criticism. Players looking to blame their shortcomings on teammates or the coach generally have a shallow approach to the game. But players who take criticism well, who can admit to weaknesses in their play, are likely to improve. I liked what I heard from many of the players during those first visits. My thoughts kept returning to that visit with Bill Walton, as my confidence that this team could win steadily increased.

I knew Larry Steele as a tireless competitor and a dedicated team player who could play both at guard and forward. I looked forward to having Larry on my team after coaching against him for several years. He was warm and outgoing as he welcomed me to Portland, confirming the positive impression I had formed of him. Because of his speed, I expected to use Larry primarily as a small forward. Frustrated by the losing seasons he had spent as a Trail Blazer, Steele was quick to agree that the game plan I projected held real promise for a winning season. My good opinion of Larry Steele as a person and a player was reinforced by his willingness to abandon his starting spot as a guard to compete for a place in the lineup as a small forward. At the time I spoke with him, I really had no idea who my starters would be. I was certain, however, that Larry would give his best in whatever role he eventually played.

I held Lloyd Neal in a similarly high regard. Lloyd, who has surprising speed for a big man, looked forward to playing the running game. Lloyd's role on the team in the plans I was forming was as a big forward and backup center. He felt comfortable in either position. As with Larry Steele, I knew Lloyd would give everything he could contribute to the team's success.

By the end of my first two weeks, I had talked with all six of the Trail Blazer players living in Portland, had flown to Los Angeles to talk to several others and had spent hours reviewing game films of the previous season. Not all of these players, however, were to figure in the Blazers' plans.

Sidney Wicks and Geoff Petrie were both involved in contractual disputes. Neither was optimistic that his contractual problems would be resolved. I was not concerned with the amounts of their salary requests, nor did I want to get involved in any way with their negotiations. But I did want all the players signed and in good condition when training camp opened in September. In addition to the contract dispute, Petrie also needed knee surgery to perform at his peak of efficiency. He wouldn't have the surgery until he signed a new contract and wouldn't sign the contract because it didn't give him what he wanted. The possibility of working the matter out seemed bleak.

Wicks also felt he was entitled to more money than he was being offered. He also suggested to me that the Blazer management was paying several players more than they were worth. And, as if over-paying his teammates wasn't enough, the Blazers also offended Sidney by paying the salaries of two coaches, myself and the deposed Lenny Wilkens. "That's all money that could be going to Sidney Wicks," he stated. I thought about that for a long time; Wicks clearly didn't put much value on my services.

I didn't feel good about the chances of having Petrie signed and in good condition for camp. I was also concerned about Wicks. He didn't really seem enthusiastic about playing in Portland for another new coach. After several meetings with the Blazers' owner, Larry Weinberg, its General Manager, Harry Glickman, and with Stu Inman, the Director of Player Personnel, we decided to trade both players.

As it turned out, of the twelve players on the roster I inherited, only five remained when the season began: Bill Walton, Lionel Hollins, Lloyd Neal, Bob Gross and Larry

Steele. The rest of the team came together over the next several months—through trades and free agency, the regular NBA draft, and the ABA dispersal draft. I had identified the spots where we needed improvement in order to play the game I intended to play. Now the task was to get the players.

Lionel Hollins' speed helps make him a tough defender. Here he meets Charlie Scott in the backcourt...

...and moves quickly to recover his defensive position as Scott drives to the sideline.

My first objective in transforming the Trail Blazers into the team I wanted was getting players with speed in the backcourt. Hollins, I knew, had the ability to play pressure defense and run the fastbreak, both essential in the game I would coach. An unassuminng player who had had a good rookie season, Hollins impressed me with his willingness to come to Portland during the summer to observe our rookie camp. He was attentive at the practices, asking intelligent questions about what I was doing. Lionel also came to Los Angeles for a week to work out with our rookie team. Few NBA veterans are willing to relinquish their summer time as Lionel did. But after Hollins, we would need help. It came from three people, none of whom had played in the same backcourt before.

Dave Twardzik was originally drafted by the Blazers in 1972, but chose to play instead for the Virginia Squires in the ABA. When the Squires folded, Dave signed with the Blazers. Portland fans have learned to tolerate a little obscurity in their favorite team's draft choices, but few suspected that Twardzik was such a fine overall player. Dave could—and can—penetrate, shoot a high percentage from the field, defend tenaciously, and satisfy the desire of open teammates to get the ball.

I knew very little about Dave, however, when I came to the Blazers. He had been signed before I took the job. But Stu Inman knew a lot about him. "He is your type of player," said Stu. "You'll love him." Stu, as it turned out, was right. I didn't think so when I first saw Dave play, but he proved himself at fall camp. Dave has an exceptional court sense, particularly in his instinct for leaving his man to go for the steal of a pass. With Twardzik and Hollins the Blazers had, I believed, two guards to play pressure defense, handle the ball and run the break.

John Davis was obtained through the annual NBA draft of college players. Before the draft took place, I described to Stu Inman the kind of guard I wanted. He thought about it only for a moment. "You're talking about John Davis," he said. I knew John Davis by reputation as a small guard with good

Dave Twardzik, I was happy to learn, has an exceptional talent for driving to the basket.

speed, great leaping ability and a dedication to team play, but I had never seen him play. Stu said he was a hardship entry in the draft, choosing to play professional basketball after his junior year at Dayton University. He was sure Davis was the man I was after. Jack McKinney had seen Davis perform at the Olympic team tryouts and concurred with Stu's opinion. "Will he be available when we pick?" I wondered. Portland had the fifth pick in the 1976 draft. Stu's second reply was as quick as the first.

"I think John will be available in the second round."

I mulled that one for a bit. "But, Stu," I said, "our greatest need is at the guard position. If John Davis is the guy that I'm talking about, let's not take a chance on losing him." But Stu had a strategy.

Wally Walker was the player he recommended taking first, because Stu was sure that Walker would not last until the second round. Though Wally was a forward rather than a guard, we would take him as our first pick because of his exceptional potential. Portland also had the third and fifth picks in the second round. We had three aims in the first two rounds of the draft: Wally Walker, John Davis and a big forward. Walker's selection, as it turned out, was no problem; when our turn came he was there and we picked him. Then the drama began.

When it came time for us to make our first selection in the second round, I looked at Stu inquiringly. "John Davis?" I asked, though I didn't really intend it as a question.

Not yet, thought Stu. "I think John will be available for our second pick this round."

"Stu," I enjoined, "don't let's pass up this guard."

But Stu was confident. "He'll be there."

He was, of course, correct. It was a great tribute to Inman's knowledge of the draft that he would predict the selections of the other teams so accurately. We took Major Jones, a big forward who had shown flashes of brilliance during the post-season All-Star games, as our first pick in the second round.

John Davis adapted quickly to the NBA; his quickness and great leaping ability were matched by his poise and determination.

The Lakers, whose second pick was sandwiched between the Blazers' two second round picks, took Earl Tatum. We, at long last, got John Davis. Stu breathed a sigh of relief. He was later to say, "If L.A. had taken J.D., I don't think I could have looked Jack Ramsay in the face again." Davis was to more than surpass the expectations I had for him. By the end of our rookie camp that summer, it was clear to me that he had all the ingredients of a good NBA guard; not just the speed and devotion to team play, which we knew he had, but defensive ability, skill at penetrating and unusual poise for a young player. The only question remaining, I thought, was simply how long it would take for him to adapt to NBA play. This, too, was answered more quickly than I expected.

Hollins now had two companions in the backcourt, but that was not enough. When Petrie was dealt to Atlanta with Steve Hawes for their pick in the ABA dispersal draft, we needed, in addition to guards who could penetrate, another quick guard who could shoot from the perimeter. Herm Gilliam, who could fill that role well, was available. We purchased him from the Seattle Sonics that summer. We also had Larry Steele, but I was thinking of him primarily as a small forward. I felt pretty good about the backcourt. But what about the guys who would get them the ball?

The front line, of course, was anchored by Walton. We couldn't do better than that. And while we had great hopes that with his strong commitment to conditioning Bill could make it through a season without serious injury, we had to prepare for the possibility that he might only match his previous high of 55 games played—of a possible 82—in one season. Lloyd Neal had proven himself as a capable backup, and was valuable at forward as well, but the team had not been able to win consistently with Lloyd carrying the load at center. Robin Jones, a free-agent rookie who had played a year in Europe after college, was a pleasant surprise at rookie camp. He showed promise as a center who could come off the bench to give Bill a rest, but didn't impress me as someone who could take over the job for long stretches either in a single game or over several games. We were still looking for help. The ABA dispersal draft gave us the opportunity to get it.

The Blazers were scheduled to pick fifth in the dispersal draft, but Stu Inman and Harry Glickman negotiated a better pick—we got the second choice, in the deal with Atlanta. I was sorry to see Hawes go, because he was a capable NBA player who could have backed up Walton. But Atlanta's position enabled the Blazers to obtain Maurice Lucas—and we couldn't pass that up. In Lucas we got both an excellent big forward and the insurance we needed at backup center. I had remembered Bob MacKinnon, who had been my assistant at Buffalo before taking the head job at St. Louis in the ABA, speaking in glowing terms about Lucas during the year that Bob coached him. I talked to Bob again; his enthusiam about Luke's potential was undiminished. Hubie Brown, however, who had coached Luke at Kentucky, did not think as highly of him. I preferred to depend on Bob's endorsement. After acquiring Lucas, we were able to make a deal for an unhappy Sidney Wicks, who eventually went to Boston. We had, in essence, given up three quality players for Maurice Lucas—but no one has ever questioned the wisdom of that deal. Lucas became in one season the best power forward in the NBA.

I visited with Maurice later at his summer camp in the Pocono Mountains in Pennsylvania. He was less than enthusiastic about playing backup center, but thought he could do well in the big forward position. He knew he would have some adjustments to make before being comfortable with the roles I had outlined for him, so he asked me to be patient until he came around. I assured him that I would treat him fairly, according him the respect he wanted from me. I didn't know yet whether Luke or Lloyd Neal would start at big forward, but simply having the choice between those two gave me a nice feeling.

The small forward's spot in the starting lineup, as I had mentioned to Larry Steele, was also open to the player who could earn it. Bob Gross, who was in Los Angeles for the summer, was one of the two leading candidates for the job. In his rookie year Bob had shown signs of brilliance, running well and playing strongly on defense. I discovered when I met him that he was quiet, preferring to let his performance speak for him. He quickly understood the requirements of the position I outlined for him, listening carefully to everything I said. He later participated in several workouts with our rookies in the Los Angeles summer league, demonstrating his capacity to run hard in our fastbreaking offense. I thought Bob would fit well in our game plan.

Bob Gross proved ideally suited to my running game.

We still had our fifth pick to exercise in that dispersal draft. Moses Malone, a fine rebounder who played inconsistently in the ABA, was our choice. We had initially hoped to deal Malone and Wicks to Boston for Jo Jo White, but the deal never materialized. The Blazer front office had made it clear to me from the beginning that the combination of Malone's $350,000 purchase price and his high-salary contract would make it impossible for the Blazers to keep him. So Moses was traded instead to Buffalo for a first-round pick in the regular NBA draft. Buffalo then traded Malone to Houston for two first-round draft picks, even though they could have had him for one first round pick from Portland. Trades are often strange. Malone played well for the Rockets, setting a league record for offensive rebounds. After I saw what he could do in the exhibition season, I really wanted Malone to stay with us. It was unfortunate that we just couldn't afford to keep him. Despite losing Malone, however, I thought we had acquired the players we needed.

Shortly after I took the Portland job, I was able to persuade Jack McKinney to join me as the Blazers' assistant coach. Jack had played for me both in high school and at St. Joseph's College, and had assisted and then succeeded me at St. Joseph's. After eight years as the head coach there, he had been for the previous two years an assistant coach of the Milwaukee Bucks. Jack knew me and the game I wanted to coach. Being together again to plan practices, discuss play options and examine defenses was like old times. I was looking forward to the coming season with greater anticipation than for any I could remember. My enthusiasm increased as the season approached. I told Jack later, as we were leaving training camp in September, that I thought we were going to win. I knew by then how good we could be. Driving back to Portland, I reflected on the long journey that had led me to where I was. Basketball had always been important to me, but never more than now. Everything seemed right. It took a long time to get from Philadelphia to Portland, but I made it. And was I ever glad I had come.

LEARNING THE GAME

CHAPTER II

IT is not true, as some of my players have suggested, that I learned to play basketball from James Naismith. My first coach, however, did go to Springfield College, where Naismith invented the game. I played organized basketball first in a grade school league in Milford, Connecticut. We played a wide open, firehouse kind of game. Our style was set after a few early practice sessions when the coach, a Walter Matthau type whom we all called Fred, grouped his players around him. He turned to the biggest guy on the team. "Batchelor," he said, "you're the rebounder. Every time you get a rebound or take the ball I want you to throw the ball to the other end of the floor." Turning to me, he continued, "Ramsay, I want you to be there to catch the ball, drive to the basket and shoot." I rather liked that offense, and we had some early success with it. But before long the opposing team would keep a man with me as I raced for the open basket. Batchelor was soon throwing more interceptions than completions. Maybe that's when I began to think about defense winning ball games. I still remember the frustration I felt after doing all that running without getting a chance to score.

I didn't learn a whole lot about the game of basketball during that period. I just knew that I loved playing and spent hours practicing almost every day all through grade school and high school. But I had to do a lot of learning on my own. I felt that my high school coaches were more interested in activities other than basketball, though they were fine men otherwise. I wish it wasn't so, but I'm afraid that it is still often true, as it was then, that high school coaches are required to coach in order to keep their teaching jobs. My family had moved from Connecticut to the Philadelphia suburbs during my tenth grade, and I transferred to Upper Darby High School. During each of the three years I played at Upper Darby, we finished second in our league to Lower Merion. Coached by Bill Anderson, whose teams looked the same every year despite losing players to graduation, Lower Merion went on each year to win the Pennsylvania state championship. Anderson's players were well drilled basketball fundamentalists who played a passing game on offense and a tight man-to-man defense. Lower Merion's game was an impressive departure from the undisciplined style I had known in Connecticut. My Upper Darby teammates and I all wished we could play on a team with the organization and discipline Bill Anderson's teams had. We all attributed Lower Merion's success to Anderson's skill as a coach. I held him in great esteem.

When it came time to choose a college, I became interested in St. Joseph's, a small Catholic college in Philadelphia which played a major college schedule. St. Joseph's coach was Bill Ferguson, a staid, conservative man who dressed in a black suit, high starched collar and black tie. Like Bill Anderson, Ferguson was a highly regarded coach. In those days, players auditioned for scholarships. After trying out with about 25 other players in the spring of my senior year in high school, I was offered a scholarship at St. Joseph's. My real basketball education began under Ferguson.

Though he had been a high school teacher during many of the 25 years he coached at St. Joseph's, he worked full-time as a banker while I played for him. Fergie was a devout Catholic, a teetotaler, and a devoted husband and father. He was a righteous man. As one might suspect, his was a highly disciplined approach to the game. He expected his players to conform to the same rigid standards he imposed upon himself. Fergie demanded that his players be in top physical condition, insisting that they refrain from smoking, drinking or dating wild women. They were, so far as Fergie knew, exemplary in all respects. Players violating Fergie's expectations were destined to sit on the bench if they weren't cut from the squad altogether.

I like to think that my own teams have inherited some of the playing qualities I learned from Bill Ferguson. He taught us to always play to our fullest, to exhaust ourselves in pursuit of victory, to never be outhustled and to never give up. It impressed me that his teams were able to win so often with just those traits. The effort of his players was more impressive than the quality of their game. They played a loose, free-lance offense and a standard man-to-man defense. We sometimes ran up against the limitations of Fergie's free-lance offense, for he was not what one would call a basketball tactician. Once I had discovered the limits in Fergie's style of play, I wanted to learn ways to tighten the defense and run a more effective offense. Yet, the lesson that teams had a chance to win on hustle alone was indelibly etched on my mind.

I started college with the intention of doing a pre-med course. Basketball practice, I soon discovered, appealed to me more than chemistry lab. Though I did reasonably well in my classes, it occurred to me then, when I was only seventeen, that if I was choosing basketball over preparation for medical school, my attachment to basketball was a pretty serious thing. I started to think about coaching. My years at St. Joseph were interrupted, however, by my enlistment into the Navy during World War II. Because of my college education, I qualified for the Navy's V-12 program for training officers and was stationed at Villanova College.

Along with a number of other trainees, I played ball for Al Severance during my year at Villanova. Unlike Bill Ferguson, Al had definite ideas about offensive play. Al's teams ran a five-man weave, give and go offense, a style then popular in the East. Also unlike Fergie, Al was outgoing and talkative. In contrast to the aloof and formal Ferguson, Severance kept his players loose with his endless store of anecdotes. Al was a running monologue on road trips, full of reminiscenses about games and players he had coached. But our team that year, burdened by a high turnover of personnel as the Navy moved people in and out of the program, had a poor record. Al seemed to me to be biding his time until the war ended rather than coaching us in a serious way. I did, however, learn something from him about a patterned offense. After finishing the program at Villanova, I was reassigned to Asbury Park Naval Station to await an opening at Midshipman's School. While there, I played basketball with some of the best college players in the country. We played on outdoor courts every free hour we had. I enjoyed playing against these players and observing the different regional styles of play they represented. I discovered that a driving, aggressive game was always productive. I made a mental note that if I ever coached, my teams were going to have that characteristic.

I left Asbury Park in August of 1944 for Columbia Midshipman's School in New York. I played briefly for the Columbia Midshipmen on a good team that included John Lujak, the Notre Dame All-American quarterback. Lujak was a good basketball player. Before I could play many games, however, I was suspended from the team for attending a basketball practice rather than a regimental meeting.

The coach, who knew that I was practicing rather than attending the regimental meeting, backed down when confronted by his superiors. "I told all the players that regimental meetings come first," he replied to their questions regarding my absence. He had not, in fact, mentioned any such policy to us at all. I was stunned by his response. I recall how he avoided my eyes as I looked at him for some explanation of his deception. It was a distressing episode. I returned to my room, suspended from the team, restricted to the base for the remainder of my time at Columbia. How, I wondered, could that coach be so deceitful with one of his players? It was an experience that confirmed my determination to always treat my players in a straightforward and honest way.

I graduated from Columbia in December, 1944, commissioned as an Ensign in the Navy. I volunteered and trained for underwater demolition work and became a member of the UDT #30. Along with the other 29 teams, we rehearsed vigorously for an invasion of Japan. Before we got to that, however, the war ended.

I found myself in Oceanside, California, with a lot of free time while the Navy tried to figure out what to do with us specially trained frogmen now that the hostilities were over. As the recreation officer for my demolition team, I organized competition in all sports. Since my evenings were free, I tried out for and made the San Diego Dons, an AAU team. On that team was Jim Pollard, the greatest player I had ever seen. It was a great experience to practice with Pollard, who at 6'7" could play the complete game. Before I could get into game competition, however, I was assigned to a small refrigerated cargo ship in the Marshall Islands of the South Pacific. After six months, during which I became captain of the ship, I was directed to bring the ship back to the states for decommissioning. I was discharged in July, 1946, free again to complete my college education and resume playing basketball.

In the fall of 1946, I returned to St. Joseph's as a somewhat matured college sophomore. I played with moderate success for three years, having firmly resolved by the time I graduated that I wanted to coach. The opportunity came quickly, with an offer from St. James High School in Chester, Pennsylvania. I thought I had learned a lot about basketball by playing against good competition in college, but I discovered myself ill-prepared for teaching the game that I enjoyed. Playing was one thing, coaching another. I discovered I didn't really know the game nor how to teach it. The intense Philadelphia Catholic League, which fed players to the Big Five Philadelphia colleges—St. Joseph's, LaSalle, Penn, Temple and Villanova—was a demanding training ground. Only in my third and last year at St. James did my team make the league playoffs. But I learned a great deal from competing with the fine coaches who had years of experience coaching in that league. By then I was still earning the $2,400 a year—plus a $100 incentive bonus for making the playoffs—for coaching basketball and baseball and teaching health and physical education classes that I had made in my first year. I wanted to stay in coaching, but with a wife and two children, I had decided I would have to give up the profession if I couldn't find a better paying coaching job.

Fortunately, Mt. Pleasant High School in Wilmington, Delaware, desired my services as a coach and a social studies teacher at nearly twice my previous salary. I enjoyed the work at Mt. Pleasant—where I was able to turn a perennial loser into a winner each of my three years there—but my real ambition was a college coaching job. They were very difficult to come by. I wrote letters whenever I heard of an opening, but received little encouragement in response. Sometimes I got no reply at all. I worked to prepare myself for any opportunity that might arise, but I was not unhappy at Mt. Pleasant nor distressed about the possibility of staying there.

Throughout my six years of high school coaching I was also adding to my basketball background by playing professional basketball in the Eastern Basketball League. I still loved to play, I needed the money, and I learned a lot that was useful to me as a coach. My first two years in the League I played for a Harrisburg, Pennsylvania, team coached by Bill Binder, who had been an excellent player at Lehigh University. We weren't able to practice much, but Binder did well coaching us under the circumstances. We made the playoff finals in Bill's only full year of coaching. But most Eastern League teams had difficulty surviving financially in competition with the popular college teams. When the Harrisburg club folded at the end of my second season there I joined the Sunbury team in the same league.

Sunbury had a lot that had been lacking in Harrisburg, not the least of which was its longevity. Most of us players were living around Philadelphia, so we could practice once or twice a week. Our coach was a contemporary and fellow player, Stan Novak, who was to coach continuously in the Eastern League from 1949 into the current year. I learned a lot of what I know about basketball during my four years with Sunbury. Four or five of us would drive together on what were then genuinely road trips—now they're really "air trips"—to save money, which gave us a chance to talk about basketball. Most of us were high school coaches, playing both for pleasure and the extra cash. Jack McCloskey, now an assistant with the Lakers and a former Trail Blazers' head coach, was a Sunbury Mercury teammate then working as a prep coach. Stan Novak, in addition to coaching the Mercurys, coached at a suburban Philly high school. Ed Lyons was yet another coach and Sunbury teammate. Our rides together were a moveable clinic. Jerry Rullo, a member of the first Philadelphia Warrior NBA championship team, also played for Sunbury. Like several other professional athletes of that era, Rullo was unable to overcome his fear of flying. One day, as his Warrior teammates boarded a plane for a flight to Cincinnati, Jerry was so overwhelmed by anxiety that he hid in a phone booth until the plane had departed. Quitting the Warriors, he joined the earthbound Mercurys, adding his knowledge of the game and the example of his skilled and fiercely competitive style to our mobile coaches' clinic.

My appetite for basketball wasn't easily sated. Even while coaching at St. James and playing in the Eastern League, I played for an independent team sponsored by Block's Department Store in nearby Norristown. McCloskey and I were again teammates. I had a guarantee of $15 a week, or a piece-rate of $5 a game if we played more than three times. I also got gas money. I was playing up to six games a week. The Block's team played in gyms and recreation halls all over Philadelphia, and occasionally in a preliminary game for the Warriors. I stayed in good shape. I had to, because the other teams always keyed on McCloskey and me. They didn't use much finesse to try to stop us either. Elbows and punches were thrown more than once in the extremely physical game we played. I survived one year on that regimen of concentrated basketball, giving it up when I took the Mt. Pleasant job.

In the midst of all this playing and coaching, I was taking graduate courses at the University of Pennsylvania. In retrospect, I don't know how I managed it all. The Sunbury and Block's schedule began in November. On the days Sunbury played, I would teach during the school day, practice the

St. James' team from 3:00 to 5:00, then leave to meet my teammates at the Valley Forge entrance to the Pennsylvania Turnpike. We would all gather in one car and head for Reading, Lancaster, or wherever the game was scheduled. Returning after the game, we'd get home between one and three in the morning. Before a Block's game I would dash home to our small apartment for a bite to eat, drive to Philadelphia, play, and then drive home. My courses at Penn were usually on Thursday evenings and Saturday mornings, so I scheduled my coaching duties around them. I studied mostly late at night or during free periods at St. James.

Sunbury played at least twice but usually not more than three times a week. We got a set figure for playing on the road—mine was $40.00 a game—and a split of the gate at home. Each of the eight Mercurys could make $75.00 on a sold-out game, so we were careful always to count the house during warmups. Sell-out crowds were inspiring in more ways than one, and we seldom lost at home. When St. James began its games in December, I had to miss an occasional Sunbury game because of scheduling conflicts. The high school schedule was finished by early March, however, so I didn't have to miss the Eastern League playoffs, which often lasted into April. Once the season was over I could concentrate on my graduate studies. I managed to complete my M.A. in guidance in my third year at St. James. Determined to advance myself professionally, I was already committed to going on for my doctorate whenever conditions permitted it. I had the responsibility of a young and growing family. I was making a little extra money playing the game I loved, but I was looking ahead for any opportunity that might arise. My chance to coach a college team finally came, but in a most unexpected way.

In the spring of 1955, when the baseball A's were still in Philadelphia, I was relaxing at a game one night with some of my colleagues from Mt. Pleasant High. Quite by accident, I ran into the Reverend Joseph M. Geib, S.J., the moderator of athletics at St. Joseph's. I knew him only slightly, since he had come to St. Joseph's after I graduated. We chatted about basketball in general, the play of the St. Joseph's teams in the years since I had graduated, and about my coaching career. It was, I thought, just polite conversation between casual acquaintances. But Father Geib then casually let fall that he was considering a coaching change at St. Joseph's. My heart literally jumped. Could this be my chance? Bill Ferguson had retired in 1952, leaving a record of achievements his successor, John McMenamin, had been unable to match. As is usually the case, the coach bears the responsibility when his team isn't meeting expectations. McMenamin was also working full-time for the Philadelphia Parks Department, leading Father Geib to believe that the coaching job needed someone who could give it his full attention.

A couple of days after our chance encounter, Father Geib called to ask if I might be interested in the head coaching job at St. Joseph's. More than simply interested, I was elated at the prospect. A few days later, following a formal interview, Father Geib called to offer me the job. In accepting St. Joseph's offer I relinquished the security of tenure at Mt. Pleasant for a one-year contract paying me $3,000 less in salary, but I wanted a college coaching job so badly I would have worked for nothing had I another source of income. I have never questioned my decision and that first year at St. Joseph's was exhilarating.

I was confident about my prospects when I took the St. Joseph's job, perhaps surprisingly so for someone who had only six years of high school coaching experience. But I had studied the game thoroughly, cramming as much into myself as I possibly could during my years as a coach. I had applied many theories in high school competition that I felt would be effective in college play. I had watched college games at every opportunity, "coaching" the teams from the stands or from my living room chair if I was watching a game on TV. I attended clinics given by eminent coaches and borrowed their game films.

The Sunbury "coaching clinics" were as invaluable as anything I had done to prepare myself. Jack McCloskey and I both felt that we were ready for college coaching. It wasn't brash boasting. We were quietly confident we could do the job. Jack's chance came first, as an assistant at the University of Pennsylvania. My opportunity at St. Joseph's came the next year. I just knew I could succeed.

McCloskey called me the night before the official announcement of my appointment at St. Joseph's was made. He had heard rumors about the possibility of my getting the job. The St. Joseph's publicist had asked me not to tell anyone about it before the press conference, at which I would be publicly named St. Joseph's head coach. But McCloskey wanted to know. "Is it true?" he shouted into the phone.

"Is what true?" I asked trying to conceal my excitement.

"Do you have the St. Joe's job?"

I paused, thinking about my commitment not to divulge anything until the next day. But I couldn't keep it from Jack.

Yes, I told him, I have the job.

"Jesus Christ," he muttered. There was a long silence. "Jesus Christ," once more. Then he hung up. I understood him. His invocation was reverent rather than profane, an acknowledgement that I had made it. It was the sort of breathless exclamation one makes upon hearing that a loved one, of whom it is certain that he has gone to heaven, has passed away. The next day I met Jack in Philadelphia. He spoke excitedly about my prospects, thinking that St. Joseph's could have a fine team. He was right.

The Big Five's inauguration of doubleheaders at the Palestra coincided with my first year at St. Joseph's. The intra-city rivalries were intense. Temple, coached then by the crafty Harry Litwack, was ranked nationally among the top three teams all season. My St. Joseph's team finished with a 23 and 6 record, winning the Big Five championship and finishing third in the National Invitational Tournament. McCloskey, of course, was assisting at Pennsylvania. Al Severance was still coaching at Villanova, while Jim Pollard, with whom I had played briefly at San Diego, coached LaSalle. It was like a reunion of old basketball friends. We competed fiercely against one another, but retained a genuinely mutual respect for each other that assured fair and cleanly contested games.

The Big Five's popularity provided it with a good supply of local players, so there was much less emphasis on recruiting then, and more attention to the development and refinement of offenses and defenses and to the techniques of teaching. There was a true commitment to *coaching*, in other words, rather than to the assemblage of an all-star cast of players. I remember well sitting up late in coffee shops during the coaches' conventions held at the NCAA finals, discussing every aspect of basketball. Great coaches like Hank Iba, Adolf Rupp and John Wooden shared their ideas with us lesser known coaches anxious to learn our craft. How to recruit blue-chippers was not a prominent subject. It was not that any of us felt we could win without good players, but rather that the surest route to success was in coaching—and I mean really coaching, not just putting all-star players on the floor. I wanted good players who were willing to abandon their personal achievements for the benefit of the team. Player talent includes traits like diving for loose balls, blocking out at the defensive boards, chasing after the player going for an open lay-up, hitting the open man on offense—it is not just scoring. I was able to obtain players with that kind of talent at St. Joseph's and never looked upon recruiting as a big factor. It involved observing the local high school competition, determining which players could play my game, getting them to apply and offering them the aid they would need to attend. My teams were comprised mostly of players from the Philadelphia Catholic League.

I remember my years at St. Joseph's with great fondness. My first year was sufficiently successful to induce Yale University to offer me its head coaching job, which in turn inspired a superior offer from St. Joseph's. My coaching salary more than doubled in a year—to the magnificent sum of $7,000. My extra teaching duties increased my earnings to over $10,000. Life was beautiful. We had moved with our four children to a residential section of Philadelphia that my wife, Jean, liked and I was doing what I wanted to do, coaching and teaching at a college. I stayed at St. Joseph's, first as coach and then as both coach and director of athletics, for eleven years. During that period my teams won more games than those of any major college. I was proud of their success.

During this time I continued to build on my basketball theories, particularly regarding defense. My first St. Joseph's teams employed a combination zone and man-to-man defense, supplemented by full- and half-court zone presses. I found, however, that the nation's best teams—the winners of the NCAA and National Invitational Tournaments—used tough man-to-man as their basic defense, mixing in some pressure formations. I concluded that my teams would have to be stronger defensively to contend for a national championship.

I particularly admired the University of California teams of Pete Newell. Borrowing films of the NCAA Tournament games played by Newell's championship team, I studied its aggressive, restrictive defense. It seemed to allow no offensive openings at all. Without the talent of the Cincinnati team of Oscar Robertson or the West Virginia team of Jerry West, Newell's team beat both of them with great defense and disciplined offense. I liked my fastbreak offense better than a patterned style, but saw ways to strengthen my defensive game. During the summer months, I pored over those films and others I had acquired to arrive at the defensive principles whose use improved the play of my final St. Joseph's teams. My basic defense now was man-to-man. Making this transition was of great value to me when I started coaching in the NBA, where the rules require man-to-man defense. I did retain the zone presses, however, which I continue to use.

My offensive game was revised less dramatically. The greatest change was to incorporate a postman, usually positioned at the foul line, to use primarily as a screener. I wanted to develop an offense that would free guard cutters through an open lane. The cutters found they could get open more easily by rubbing their men off a stationary postman than by simply

I still use the trapping defenses I developed at St. Joseph's. Here Gross (guarding the dribbler), Lucas (#20) and Hollins (opposite Lucas) prepare to double team, while Twardzik hangs back to pick off a lob pass.

cutting through the open lane. That idea generated a very effective shuffle-cut style of attack. I still use the principle of the stationary postman, but have found that placing him in the low post better utilizes his passing and shooting skills. Through all my years in coaching, I have worked to refine my style of play.

The only dark moment of that eleven-year period came in 1961 when three of my players conspired with gamblers to shave points in three early season games. Their collusion was not revealed until after the season ended. The revelation made meaningless an outstanding season in which St. Joseph's had a 25-5 record and finished third in the NCAA tournament. I was crushed. I could not believe my players could do such a thing. But they had been induced by the lure of money and the gamblers' premise that they weren't being asked to lose—"Just don't win by so much." St. Joseph's had established a fine tradition of winning achieved through team spirit—emphasizing all-out individual effort and togetherness to achieve victory. Yet three players had violated that proud tradition, putting themselves first. It was a sad and shocking period for college basketball.

I did a great deal of soul-searching. Had my own obsession with basketball and my determination to play the optimum game every game been too much for my players to accept? Had I closed my eyes to their needs as individuals in my zeal to have a great basketball team? Was I really using these players and the team to further myself as a coach? I pondered the perplexing questions flooding my guilt-laden conscience. I considered resigning from the job that I had sought so fervently. The college president and Father Geib urged me to stay on, saying it would be a disservice to leave the players who remained. They also expressed confidence that I was the person most able to correct the distasteful situation that had developed. It wasn't in my makeup to quit when things didn't go well. I determined to do a better job, especially in the area of personal communications, to restore credibility to my team and to the college game of basketball.

The determination and dedication of my next season's St. Joseph's team did much to remove whatever smear may have remained to taint the Hawks' image. At the conclusion of practice the night before that season's opening game, the team captain, Jim Lynam, a Dave Twardzik-type guard, drew an imaginary line with his foot in the back court of the opposition. "Chang," he called to a teammate, "they don't get past here." Lynam was prophetic. The opposing guards had a tough time getting the ball out of their own backcourt and St. Joseph's blistered Bucknell to begin another tournament-bound season.

Near the end of my eleventh year at St. Joseph's I began to have vision problems with my right eye. The condition was diagnosed as an edema on the retina, which clouded my sight. I lost depth perception and was unable to read from that eye. Ophthalmologists told me that it was a condition that frequently accompanied stress. They advised me to relax more. That was hard for me to do while coaching, so when Irv Kosloff, the owner of the Philadelphia 76ers, asked if I would become the team's General Manager, I agreed. I took the job in late August; by October my eye condition had cleared up.

I really thought I had finished my coaching career. The 76ers had a capable coach in Alex Hannum, the team was strong and I had signed a three-year contract as General Manager. We won the NBA championship that first year and I thought my future was in front office management. But I was naive to the ways of the NBA. After two years, Hannum quit, saying, "I can't take that big guy (Wilt Chamberlain) anymore." In searching for a replacement for Hannum I spoke with many coaches. Bill Sharman, who had done a fine job with the San Francisco Warriors, was not interested because he was going with the new ABA team in Los Angeles. Frank McGuire did not want to leave his college coaching job at South Carolina. John Kundla, who had coached NBA championship teams with the Minneapolis Lakers, wasn't excited about coaching Chamberlain and opted to remain at the University of Minnesota. Earl Lloyd, a former NBA standout with Detroit, was interested but his lack of coaching experience bothered me.

Then Wilt Chamberlain approached me about becoming a player-coach, like Bill Russell was then at Boston. He said he would do it if I would assist him with the technical work. After some deliberation, I decided that Wilt's suggestion might work out. I thought Wilt's determination to have a winning record as a coach would inspire him to play well enough to assure it. I could provide the necessary technical knowledge to the team. I had had two years to observe closely the 76ers under Alex Hannum, as well as the other NBA teams. I had developed ideas on how to play that I thought would be effective in the NBA. I had also discovered that professional players were no different than those at any other level in wanting coaching direction. I was somewhat surprised and pleased to discover that the pros wanted systematic treatment, liked to be worked hard and, above all, wanted each player to be treated equally and fairly. They wanted and respected firm treatment.

My interest in coaching aroused once more, I obtained Kosloff's okay to firm up the agreement with Wilt. It was going to be player-coach Wilt Chamberlain and General Manager-assistant coach Jack Ramsay. But, following a trip to the West Coast, Wilt suddenly had a change of heart. Not only was he not interested in being player-coach, he was, in his words, "never going to play for Philly again." He demanded to be traded to the L.A. Lakers; if not, he would jump the NBA and join the new ABA team in Los Angeles.

So, we worked out a trade with the Lakers that would bring Darrell Imhoff, Archie Clark and Jerry Chambers to the 76ers in exchange for Chamberlain. Because the 76ers had Luke Jackson, a strong, young 6'9" center-forward who appeared to have a great career ahead of him, I thought the deal was a good one under the circumstances. If Wilt had jumped to the ABA, the Sixers would have got nothing in return. Imhoff would be an excellent backup. The rest of the team was solid—Chet Walker and Billy Cunningham at forwards, Clark, Hal Greer, Wally Jones and Matt Guokas at guards. But they didn't have a coach. Kosloff asked if I would coach the team—at least for a year—until another coach could be obtained. I agreed and was back in coaching.

I liked that team. It was similar to the present Portland team. We had a fine training camp. The players seemed to like the work I had them do and I felt good about our progress. We started the season well. Then, in our twenty-fifth game, Luke Jackson tore his achilles tendon in a game against Phoenix. Not only was Luke finished for that season, he was never able to regain his previous level of performance. We were 18-7 at that time. Imhoff came on to do a super job and we finished 55 and 27. But in the playoffs we were not strong enough to beat Boston without Jackson.

Despite our losing in the playoffs, however, I found coaching in the NBA a fascinating experience. The best players in the world were competing through 82 regular-season games, struggling for a place in the playoffs. And nothing could match the excitement of the second season, the championship playoffs. It was the greatest challenge one could hope for in basketball coaching. So I set out in pursuit of the Holy Grail of professional coaches, the Walter Brown Trophy, emblematic of NBA and world basketball supremacy.

The quest took me through three more seasons at Philadelphia, during which I constantly sought to overcome the lack of a dominant center before I did something I don't remember ever having done before. I gave up! I felt I just couldn't do the job in Philadelphia. So, I resigned. After considering several offers, I decided to take the coaching job at Buffalo, mostly because of its General Manager, Eddie Donovan, whom I had long admired and with whom I got along well.

Following a disastrous first season in Buffalo, Eddie and I revamped the club and it had three fine seasons. Eddie, however, had a falling out with owner Paul Snyder and left during my third season there. The mutual disenchantment extended to Snyder and me the following year. I decided I could no longer coach under the prevailing conditions.

During the playoffs that final season in Buffalo, Stu Inman called me from Portland. Would I be interested, Stu wondered, if the coaching job at Portland was available? My first thought was of Bill Walton. I really liked his game. I told Stu that I would be interested, and we arranged to meet in Buffalo. We talked theory, practice procedures, handling of players and many related basketball topics. I enjoyed the meeting. Stu said he would get back to me after the playoffs. My Buffalo team was eliminated by Boston, Snyder and I had our parting of the ways and I started to explore new coaching opportunities—but hoping the Portland job would materialize. Several weeks later, after meetings with Larry Weinberg, the club president, I agreed to take the job as the Trail Blazers' coach. The most enjoyable year in my coaching life was about to begin.

PART II: THE COACH'S ART

THE TEAM GAME

CHAPTER III

COACHING is a means of self-expression. Successful coaches, like artists, have a characteristic style. No coach lacking a firm sense of what he wants to accomplish through his team can succeed. A coach's philosophy will guide him in selecting the kind of game he wants to play, the expectations he has of his players, and the manner in which he will teach his game. A coach's personality, and hence the character of his team, is reflected in his philosophy of the game. This is not a matter of innovation or of creating some formidable new defense or a novel offense. There are no original ideas left in basketball, given the fixed nature of the game. You can field five players at a time, who, within the established limits of a 94-by-50 feet court, try to put a ball slightly more than nine inches in diameter through an 18-inch hoop placed exactly ten feet above the floor, while simultaneously preventing the other team from doing the same thing. It is within this fixed form that a coach must express himself. Determining his philosophy is, therefore, a coach's primary task; he must decide, before anything else, what it is he wants to say of himself through the game.

As with any artist, a coach's style will evolve. He borrows freely from his playing experience, if any, and from predecessors and colleagues, refining his game. But the game he plays must be his own. Simply imitating the style of a successful coach is not the same thing as determining one's own coaching philosophy. Good coaching begins with self-scrutiny, which, in turn, leads to a selection of a playing style. And once that style has been honestly determined, a coach can begin the task of translating it into practice. If he has selected and translated well, his team will manifest his ideas when it takes the floor to play. It will be clearly recognizable as his team. For myself, if I am doing my job well, my team will play "Ramsay basketball."

PLAYER MOTIVATION AND TEAM PSYCHOLOGY

No team can win in any sport without skillful athletes. Desire alone can't substitute for talent. A highly motivated player with insufficient talent just can't do the job, no matter how hard he tries. However, a highly skilled but poorly motivated player can, with proper coaching, learn to integrate his skills into a team's overall style of play. A coach must first, therefore, select players who have the skills to play his game. Given a choice between two players of roughly equal skill, one would of course choose the better motivated. But the ability of a player to perform in his position is the first criterion I use in evaluating personnel. The best attitudes in the world won't help win ball games if they're not accompanied by a fundamental competence in the game. Assessing players, like every other part of the coach's art, derives from the selection of a style of play.

In my game, I need players at every position with speed, quickness, strength, and stamina. I need tenacious defenders, a couple of strong rebounders, good passers, quick small forwards, driving guards and a postman. The man in the post is the hub in my team concept, both on offense and defense. He should be a strong defender, capable of blocking shots, rebounding, and making the outlet pass. He must also be able to pass, shoot, screen and rebound on offense. In essence, he is a Bill Walton. But for the postman to play his game to the fullest, he needs the support of skilled players at the other positions. I need also to have guards who can play defense, handle the ball and run on offense, and forwards who can defend, run and rebound. Having defined the skills I need at each position, I can then look for players to fill them.

Bill Walton's shot blocking is a great asset in my fastbreak game.

I seldom have an opportunity to watch college players perform, so like other NBA coaches I depend heavily on the appraisals of team scouts. In order for them to know what I'm looking for in the players we will draft, I have to inform them of my needs as clearly as possible. Sometimes this doesn't happen. When I was coaching in Philadelphia, the 76ers were in desperate need of a center to replace the injured Luke Jackson. My requirements for a postman then were the same as they are now. At a meeting to discuss the draft, I discovered that our scouts were high on a player whom they described as a "Wes Unseld type." I remember thinking, "If this guy can play like Wes Unseld, we definately should take him." So we drafted him, signed him to a multi-year, high salary-contract, and brought him to training camp. Unfortunately, he only looked like Unseld. He sure couldn't play like Wes. He's never played in an NBA game. The way to avoid something like that ever happening again is to make sure that everyone involved in scouting knows exactly what I expect of the players we need.

Part of the trouble in Philadelphia was that we just didn't have a good scouting operation. The head scout's experience was more in baseball than basketball, and his staff was filled with other baseball men. The scouts for the other teams found this amusing. "Do you think we can make the double play?" they would ask the Philadelphia scout of a player he was watching. "Does he have a major league arm?" Philadelphia's scouting then was not highly regarded in the NBA. Scouting, and the draft for which it is preparation, are much too important to leave to a haphazard procedure.

Occasionally a player with the skill to play in the NBA simply won't have the strength of character to survive the demands professional basketball makes on players. Not only is the schedule long and arduous, but the fans and press are sometimes cruelly critical of a player's performance. As not everyone can handle this pressure, it's important to evaluate a player's personal qualities as well as his playing skills. How can one measure the character traits essential to success in the NBA? It's not always easy. The traditional method of talking to scouts, coaches, and the players themselves yields valuable information, but it's time-consuming and not always dependable. A player's college coach, for example, may let his enthusiasm for a player cloud his judgment. A more reliable tool, I've found, is a multiple choice test developed by the Institute of Athletic Motivation, called the Athletic Motivation Inventory, or the AMI. It has a high predictive value in measuring the personality traits associated with successful athletes. A player scoring well on this test will generally have a strong desire to win, a belief in self-assertion, and a determination to improve. He will be willing to accept responsibility for what he does, to assume a leader's role, and to maintain confidence in his ability. He will be emotionally stable, able to bounce back from adversity. He will, finally, be comfortable with his teammates and respectful of his coaches. Any player both skilled and possessing in abundance the qualities the AMI is designed to measure has a good chance of making it in the NBA. Unfortunately, however, very few players are given the AMI before the draft takes place. Discovering that a player isn't what was expected after he's signed and in camp is a frustrating experience.

Building the Team

Once the players have been selected, it is the coach's job to mold them into a team. That process begins, as does all good coaching, with a clear definition of each player's role in meeting the team's objectives. There are three levels of interaction tightly woven into the fabric of a successful team. Each player must first know his position in the context of the team's overall style of play. Having a thorough understanding of the functions of every position is a part of knowing one's own position well. The guards know what is expected of the forwards, for example, just as they both know what playing in the postman's position entails. In addition to his playing position, each player fills another role on the team; he starts, or he comes off the bench. Though they may play fewer minutes, the bench players are no less significant to the team than the starters. No one is on the team simply to fill out the roster. Finally, each player has personal needs to which the coach must be sensitive. Each of these levels of interaction is important in the process of building a team.

Most players want to do well, but in order for them to play up to their ability they need direction. It is the coach's job to supply it. Setting attainable goals for each player is an essential part of good coaching. Players need to know exactly what's expected of them, both at practice and during games. Defining the responsibilities of each position, and drilling the players in them, helps set reasonable goals. The man who plays in the ballhandler's position, for example, has to be a good ballhandler. He doesn't have to rebound, he doesn't have to score a lot, but he must be able to control the ball. However obvious this may seem, it must be made explicit. Expecting a poor ballhandler to control the flow of the offensive attack puts an unreasonable expectation on that player. A player who neither knows what is expected of him nor has had an opportunity to practice his position can't perform well. But players who know what to do, and who have had a chance to practice what they know, will have confidence in themselves in a game. A player who is confident in his game, who wants to test it in competition, is a well motivated player.

I don't think personal goals beyond meeting the responsibilities of one's playing position have much meaning in basketball. Players trying to achieve high averages—in scoring, rebounding, or anything else—have little attraction for me. Team goals are the only ones that really matter. Even high figures in apparently unselfish statistical categories can be misleading. A player with a lot of rebounds, for example, might be leaving his man open for easy jump shots while he hangs around the basket to pull down missed shots. Nor do a large number of assists by one player necessarily indicate selfless play. A player may be holding onto the ball too long, slowing down the offense, rather than hitting the open man in front of him. What finally matters is who wins and loses. And if we win, the team statistics will come out right.

I don't want my team outrebounded. The players who have the job of rebounding know they must play harder if we are getting fewer rebounds than our opponent. If we're giving up a lot of assists, we need to play better defense. The guards, for example, may be allowing too much penetration, or their center may be getting the ball too easily in a good position to pass. We may be switching poorly. Conversely, if we're not getting enough assists then everyone isn't involved in the offense. But it is the team statistics that matter, not individual ones. Each player knows what is expected of him, knows what adjustments to make in his play if we're trailing our opponent in assists or rebounds.

The Trail Blazers were once struggling in a game with the New Jersey Nets. We weren't getting the ball up the floor rapidly, we weren't filling the passing lanes. We weren't applying good defensive pressure. After looking at the stat sheet at half time, I remarked to Jack McKinney, "We have a team total of seven assists." I pointed this out to the players, all of whom knew what was required to generate more assists. I didn't accuse any particular player, indicting instead the play of the team. They got the message. In the second half we were more aggressive, we rebounded and filled the lanes, and ended with nineteen assists in the second half. We also won.

When we do play well, I want the players to know that their efforts are appreciated. I will praise them privately, before the team or in the press. We all need a little recognition when we do something well. It's a nicely turned circle. The team plays well when each player is performing well in his position. And each player will perform well if he knows what's expected of him, if he's encouraged to practice what he does well, if he's tutored on the weak points of his play, and if he's rewarded for a job well done.

It's important to know every player well, to realize when someone needs a boost or a push. I have many personal conversations with each player during the season. It may be in an airport or on a bus, or in a hotel coffee shop. Wherever it occurs it gives me a chance to recognize a player's worth and to acknowledge his importance to the team. I want to know if a player has something on his mind, whether it's a problem in his personal life or a question regarding his place on the team. If he's unhappy with something, I want to know about it. Every player needs to feel important to the team, from the starters to the last reserve.

In the course of a long NBA season, every player will make a significant contribution at one time or another, but keeping players ready who are seeing little action is not always easy. Part of keeping a player ready is simply explaining to him the role he has on the team. A good bench player knows what he's supposed to do and why he's doing it. How do I keep bench players ready? I include every player in every game plan, first of all, reviewing the assignments and matchups as thoroughly for the substitutes as for the regulars. I use the bench players when the game action calls for it, and they know that I will do so. If a player isn't capable of playing in critical situations, he shouldn't be on the team. Just as the starters know that they will be substituted for at some point in the game, the bench players know that their job is to maintain the game plan while the regulars rest.

I also give the short-minute players extra attention in practice, working with them to improve their skills. In practice the day after a hard game, particularly, the players who played least know they'll have the hardest workout. While the regulars recuperate, the other players may go two-on-two full court, followed by some personalized instruction. Whatever technique I use, its purpose is to demonstrate to each player his value to the team and keep him at performance readiness. A good bench player responds to that treatment.

In the 1976-77 playoffs, Corky Calhoun, playing big forward behind Maurice Lucas and Lloyd Neal, did not play at all in the series with Los Angeles. A lesser player might have got down on himself, frustrated at not having had the opportunity to play against a team which had cut him before the season began. But Corky, despite whatever disappointment he felt, never faltered. All during the Los Angeles series, and then in preparation for the 76ers, Corky worked hard at practice. I made him do extra running, urging him to keep in shape. I told him to keep ready, that I would use him when the need arose. And need him I did. Julius Erving was great in our series with the 76ers, but less than he might have been because of Corky Calhoun's defensive play. I don't think we would have beaten Philadelphia had not Corky been willing and able to prepare himself for an opportunity he couldn't even be certain would arise. Like all good team players, Corky Calhoun put the team above himself—and for his willingness to do so now wears an NBA World Championship ring.

Personal Motivation

Coaching is a private act sometimes performed in public places. Coaching in a game is only a part of the job, but it's the part that finally counts the most. A losing coach is, sooner than not, a former coach. If the team goes badly, the coach is responsible. But if the team wins, the players deserve and get the bulk of the credit. I like it that way. I know when I've done my job well, and savor the satisfaction it brings. No one can ever take that away. But coaching is an insecure profession, requiring of its practitioners a capacity to withstand external pressures while leading a team through a long, demanding season. A coach has to have a firm sense of himself, sustained by intense powers of concentration. I hate to lose, but I know that once a game is over I have to put it out of my mind in order to prepare for the next one. I have to minimize the depth of my disappointment, disguising it from my players because it's infectious. I have to lead them by example as well as by precept. I get mad when officials make bad calls, but I can't let my anger distract me from the game. Maintaining my ability to concentrate, to focus all of my attention on the task at hand, is part of my own responsibility as a coach.

I keep physically fit in order to stay on top of the mental stress which coaching invariably produces. Jumping rope, swimming and bicycling provide me with exercise during the season. The activity itself is a good release, and it helps me to get six to eight hours of daily rest. It keeps me focused on the job at hand, capable of disregarding the trivial while attending to what matters. I try to eat well, too, limiting myself to two meals a day but eating green vegetables, fish and dairy products in abundance. I drink fruit juices, milk, tea and a bit of coffee, and keep my weight down where I want it while eating enough to maintain my energy level. Vitamins and protein supplements round out my diet.

I can't always sleep when I want, no matter how well I take care of myself. Sometimes a game is so stimulating that I can't get to sleep at all once it's over. I don't make a great virtue of regularity or rigid schedules for myself, but I do follow a simple basic rule to guide my daily habits: I sleep when I'm tired, I eat when I'm hungry, and I exercise when I'm rested. When I'm physically fit, I can give all of myself every day to my job. I also have enough faith in myself to believe that when I'm doing my job well, the results will speak for themselves.

THE PHILOSOPHY OF COACHING

The philosophy determines every aspect of practice, the objectives of meetings, and finally the game plan. It is the cement which binds every activity of a coach and his team, linking practice drills to game performance. The preparation of a team begins with planning practices, for it is on the practice floor that teaching the game occurs. The importance of planning practices can't be overstated. A practice session's objectives, expressed in a practice plan, must be determined in advance—and in detail. The players need to know the point of what they will be doing. Posting the practice schedule in the locker room, I've found, is a good technique. It informs the players both about what we will be doing and how long we will take doing it. I can't always post a schedule for the Blazers, particularly on the road, but I will always summarize for the players what they can expect in practice.

Brief meeting of players: 2-5 minutes--to give objectives and activities of practice.

Stretch outs: 20 minutes--stretching to loosen and increase flexibility potential of muscle groups pertinent to basketball activity.

Warm-up: 10 minutes--three-man full court passing and short shooting drills, stressing fundamental ball handling, lay-up, jump shot, rebounding, and organized three-on-two and two-on-one fastbreak.

Defensive Emphasis: 15 minutes--break down defensive requirements:
1. Three-man plays
   a. Offensive play: guard, forward, center pick and roll.
      Defensive objectives: Deny guard reception of ball from forward. Force offensive player with ball to baseline. Defender of center to play on baseline side of screener. Defender of driver to play on mid-court side of opponent.

   b. Offensive play: Guard, forward split off low post.
      Defensive objectives: Defenders on cutters drop toward post after he has received pass; move with opponents to the point of screen, then switch.

   c. Offensive play: Forward screen down for guard on baseline--pass from high-post center.
      Defensive objectives: Forward defender open space between self and offensive forward to allow defensive guard to move past the screener without switching and to prevent reception of pass. Defensive forward then plays between his man and ball to prevent post-up position. Defensive center pressures pass from high post position.

Offensive Emphasis: 15 minutes--half-court, three man movement concentrating on screening action with post man and passing under pressure.

Offensive Play: Side court player (guard or forward) passes to player at top of circle then cuts off low post center to receive return pass. Passer is defended tightly and may not dribble. Defenders may switch or stay with their men; offensive players respond with play to open man. (Variations of this drill allow for backdoor play through center for overplayed receiver; one-on-one drive from top of circle; post splits for two cutters; lob pass to overplayed post man; back cut pass to overplayed player moving to top of circle position.

Offensive play: Weakside cutters through lane and along baseline to receive pass from low post center. Four man drill stressing timing and screening to free cutters through open lane area.

Offensive Play: Post-up of forward, deep along lane, to receive pass from player at corner or high-post position. Stress getting position without fouling, passing ball to player with appropriate pass from either position, fake and shoot.

Offense and Defense: 15 minutes--five-man half-court work utilizing total offense against defense. Defensive team rebounds misses and takes steals for fast break opportunities. Offensive team retains possession after each score. Change teams to offense and defense and rotate players in same manner as substitutions are made in game.

Full court scrimmage: 20 point game (about 15 minutes)

Free throws and free shooting practice: 10-15 minutes.

Finish practice with full squad full-court line drill: running end line to half court, back to end line, to opposite foul line, back to end line, to opposite end line, back to end line. 30 seconds.

A typical mid-season Trail Blazer practice session

I invariably schedule defensive drills first. It's a small way to impress upon the players my belief that defense, as the key to team success, comes first. The drill work at practice, whether on offense or defense, is always made up of components of our defensive or offensive pattern. It's important to break the game down into its basic parts, explain the significance of each, and then drill, drill, drill. Once the components have been mastered, they can be fitted into the whole. A variation on this teaching strategy is building up from one to two to three to four-man plays before involving all five players. This approach also allows for individualized instruction, during which players can be taught their personal responsibilities within the context of the team's overall patterns of play.

When I'm teaching a new drill, I always walk the players through it until it's clear that each one thoroughly understands it. Then we can go full speed. But not for too long, because the tedium of repetition can interfere with learning. Fatigue affects concentration, and players need to have their full attention on what they're doing. The same principle operates in a game, so observing its effects in practice is another form of game preparation.

Players like organization, they like order, they will work hard when they see the purpose of what they're doing. When every player knows what's expected of him and why, practices will be productive. And then even hard, physically demanding sessions will be fun, building the sense of common purpose and collective affection every good team has. When players and coaches feel good about what's happening in practice, they will carry that spirit with them into games. I want every practice well organized, productive, and conducted with the same intensity and commitment as a game is played.

A coach who allows players to depart from his plan at practice can expect the same thing in a game. If it is his team, it must perform the way he expects it to. The players are the medium through which a coach expresses his philosophy. The artist must be in control of his medium, and a coach must prepare his players for their performance. Just as drills are the basic parts of a team's game, its style of play, practices, too, must reflect other demands a team will encounter in games. Teaching pace, an awareness of time and the significance of the clock, the importance of officials and score differentials, are all also a part of what practices must prepare for.

Once a team has acquired a basic competence in its style of play, it is ready to begin preparation for the game. Before a season starts, a team should be prepared for every situation that will arise in competition. It should be ready to defend against any offense or attack any defense, to adjust to any game situation. Its style of play is set, its overall game plan established. It may be a fastbreaking team or a deliberate team, a pattern team or an aggressive, pressing team. It may even be a team with multiple offensive and defensive techniques. Whatever its game, a team's style should be fixed and assimilated before the first game is played.

In competition, each team poses a unique challenge, which a game plan is designed to meet. The preparation of a game plan begins with a study of the opponent's style of play, its strengths and weaknesses. This analysis is a critical part of coaching. If an assessment of an opponent is inaccurate, the game plan will be inadequate. A sound appraisal can't be made from watching a team play only once, though this is not a problem in the NBA, where teams play often and players are often in the league for many years. Game films and videotapes are valuable aids in detecting subtle qualities in a player's game, and are often helpful in ways that even watching a game is not. I use videotape stop action to trace an individual's step-by-step moves. Opposing player habits can be detected, providing invaluable teaching aids for the defensive preparation of one's players.

The object of any game plan is to limit an opponent's opportunities to do what it does best, while carrying out one's own style of play. Game plans, therefore, can vary considerably while remaining within the limits of a particular style. In the 1977 NBA playoffs, the Trail Blazers met four teams whose styles of play greatly differed, yet we were able to play each effectively. Without abandoning our overall team plan of aggressive defense and a running, quick-action offense, we adjusted to each team in the playoffs. A review of what we did will illustrate the idea of the game plan. Let's examine our defensive strategy postion by position.

The Portland guards, who form the first line of defense for the Blazers, pressured the Los Angeles Lakers in the backcourt. We wanted to keep the great Laker center, Kareem Abdul-Jabbar, from getting the ball in the deep post. Against the Chicago Bulls, however, our guards picked up at halfcourt, concentrating on denying the guard to forward pass with which Chicago prefers to initiate its offense. Our purpose against Philadelphia was to pressure the guards with the ball so they would be unable to penetrate the top of the circle. The 76ers' response to this strategy was using its center to bring the ball upcourt, in effect making our guards' job easier. The running game of the Denver Nuggets resembles our own, so our guards were required to concentrate on retreating to the defensive zone in order to prevent the Denver fastbreak. But nothing in our *style* of play was altered to make those adjustments. Nor did the variations in the play of our forwards and center take us out of our overall game plan. Here are the adjustments we made.

Against Philadelphia, our primary object was to deny Julius Erving the ball; if he did get it, we wanted to double-team him. Our big forward was to keep George McGinnis away from the low post, but drop off him when he had the ball on the perimeter. The scoring ability of Chicago's forwards, on the other hand, made constant, tight defensive pressure on them necessary. Denver's David Thompson, who is a great scorer, got double-teamed whether he was playing guard or forward. But Paul Silas, who was not an offensive threat, had only to be kept away from the offensive board. We wanted our small forward to keep heavy pressure on the Lakers' Cazzie Russell, but our big forward was to help Bill Walton by double-teaming Abdul-Jabbar whenever he could.

Each series likewise required specific adjustments by the center. Chicago's Artis Gilmore is principally a shooter from the low post, but his back-up, Tom Boerwinkle, is primarily a passer from the medium post. So while we would try to deny Gilmore the ball in his favored position, we would allow Boerwinkle to receive it out high. Philadelphia's centers were not much of a scoring threat, so we allowed them to handle the ball while using our center to help out defensively on other players. But as Denver's starting center, Dan Issel, is an excellent perimeter shooter, our center had to go out after him. Issel's substitute, Marvin Webster, doesn't shoot well from outside but can score around the basket. We didn't want to give Webster easy access to the ball on pick-and-roll plays, or opportunities for offensive rebounds. Against Los Angeles, of course, we had to keep Kareem from getting the ball where he could turn into the lane for his nearly unstoppable skyhook. But if Kareem did get the ball, Bill wanted to force him to the baseline where our big forward could give defensive help.

So while our defensive assignments varied over the four playoff series, our basic defensive thrust was unaltered: we wanted to challenge our opponents' strengths while taking advantage of their weaknesses. Our offensive game plan, like our fundamental defensive posture, was also constant from series to series. We wanted to run the ball, carrying on our turnout offense with continuous quick-action cuts even if we didn't have a fastbreak. We stayed in the style of play established at the first day of training camp the previous September.

I have made it a practice in recent years to have workouts, usually at around noon, on the day of the game. We begin with a discussion of the game plan, emphasizing the essential characteristics of our opponent's style of play. A preview of likely match-ups also helps each player prepare for the game. Following this brief canvass, we run through our opponent's offense, stressing the overall defense we expect will be effective against it. The final portion of the hour we usually spend on a game-day workout is given over to shooting, both from the field and the free-throw line. Players need to familiarize themselves with the away-from-home court, and always take time practicing particularly on the shots they are likely to take in the game. They can study the court, the lighting, the shooting backgrounds, or any unusual markings on the playing floor. They shouldn't be strangers to a court when they go out to play a game, even on the road.

No matter how thoroughly a game plan is prepared and practiced, it can't predict everything a coach will encounter in a game. The execution of the game plan can be influenced, for example, by an injury or an exceptional game by a player on either team. Early foul trouble by a key player is always significant. All of this occurs outside the game plan, but it must be anticipated nonetheless. When the unexpected arises, the coach must be ready to adjust, to keep the action going in the direction he wants. Even a game in which nothing extraordinary happens, however, requires constant evaluation. The assistant coach can play a valuable role in assessing game situations.

The relationship between a head coach and his assistant, defining the roles each will play, must be clearly established. I like my assistant to look for signs of player fatigue on both squads, to make general observations to me about offensive movements, and to look for defensive lapses in our opponent's play which we might exploit. I want him to speak freely to me, to make his observations without hesitation. The head coach is the ultimate arbiter, but the contributions of his assistant can help put any judgment on a firmer basis.

Two questions guide the observations of a coach as he watches a game unfold: "How is the game plan being followed?" and "Is the game plan proving effective?" Examining the defensive play of the guards is the first step in answering these questions. Are the guards carrying out their defensive responsibilities? Are they putting enough pressure on the ball? Are they picking up the ball quickly enough? Are they forcing the ball in a predetermined direction? Are they preventing penetration? Are they working well together? Are they switching men properly? All of these questions must be answered in the first few minutes of a game. The play of the guards, who form the first line of defense, is critical to any game plan. If they aren't effective, the other players will have difficulty fulfilling their roles.

Once the guards' play has been assessed, the defensive play of the forwards has to be evaluated. As is the case with guards, a checklist of questions guides a coach's study of the forward's play. Is the ball side forward receiving enough pressure? Is he being denied the ball at the point he wants to receive it? Are the forwards being checked off the offensive boards? Are the forwards being restricted on their passing or driving opportunities? Answering these questions is crucial to evaluating the game plan.

The defensive play of the center is also monitored by a check list. Is the opposing center getting the ball where he wants it? Or, is he being taken out of his team's offensive pattern? These questions are no less pertinent as the game progresses. If the answers to these questions indicate a defensive breakdown, a timeout might be necessary. Substitutions might also enter the game, with specific instructions to fulfill the game plan. This may occur outside of the ordinary rotation of substitutes, which is itself a vital part of coaching.

Players need to have a feel for how long they are going to play, and an idea of when and for how long they will be rested. Bench players in particular need to know when they are likely to enter a game, as well as a general idea of the length of time they will play. There are exceptions, of course, to any general rules for playing time. If a player is going extremely well, a coach will want to play him a bit longer than normal; a player not doing well should expect shorter minutes. Players coming off the bench should try to get into the flow as quickly as possible. This takes a special kind of preparation and concentration. Not everyone is good off the bench, but any player in that role should realize his responsibility. Good bench players always watch carefully when they're not playing, and adjust rapidly to the action when they enter the game.

The details of the offensive game plan must also be attended. If the defense is working well, the offense is also likely to operate effectively. But just as with the defense, the offense requires continuous evaluation. Is the ball moving quickly enough from one end of the floor to the other? If the fastbreak is required, are the rebounders getting the ball to the outlet men? Are the outlet men in position to receive the pass? Are the lanes being filled quickly? Is the break being carried through or are the players simply running to the end line and stopping? Is there enough player movement and passing action to test the opponent's defense? If one's team is giving up fast breaks to the opponent, is it because the offense is not being carried through completely? Are offensive players out of position when shots are taken so that there is not proper backcourt coverage? All of these questions need constant attention during a game. If the answer to very many is "No," then a timeout or substitutions will probably be necessary.

Timeouts are also important to the tempo of the game. Since the team ahead at the end of the game, and not the one leading after the first, second or third periods, is the winner, keeping track of the pace of a game is vital. Here, too, questions need asking. Is the game tempo overall the one we want? If we're fastbreaking, have we established the tempo of the running game? If the answer to these questions is "Yes," then we're likely to do better as the game progresses. An opponent unaccustomed to a running, pressure game will suffer the effects of losing stamina in the late stages of the game. Using substitutes carefully can help dictate tempo. Constantly running the ball at an opponent's offensive star, for example, might tire him enough so that his scoring suffers. If he gives up more points than he scores, he has not been effective. In this regard, keeping track of an opponent's traveling schedule can also provide an edge. Is he coming off a hard game, or at the end of a long road trip? Conversely, when we're on a long road trip I may play everyone for shorter minutes to sustain the tempo I want.

Halftime

Halftime is an opportunity to assess the first half and plan any variations necessary in the second. It lasts only fifteen minutes. While the players are resting, getting something to drink and having the trainer check their injuries and ailments, I confer with my assistant to evaluate the first half. After four or five minutes, during which the players relax and put on their warm-up suits, I begin a five-minute discussion of the game, reviewing what has happened and previewing any changes I expect to make. I diagnose any problems we may be having, outlining the adjustments we may need to make. Substitutes likely to play more, or even to see action for the first time in the second half, are told what to expect. They can then use the five-minute warm-up on the court before the second half to prepare themselves. By the time the players return to the court, they should be concentrating on the jobs they will have during the final quarters of play.

I also study the stat sheets at halftime, looking for any significant figures on team and individual rebounds and assists, shooting percentages and personal fouls. Any less than five fouls by a starting player in the first half I regard as insignificant. Good players can play a half with five fouls. I think coaches too frequently let the foul situation dictate their strategy. I would rather play my key players, even at the risk of their fouling out, in order to stay with the game plan. If, however, as is often the case, a player is both in foul trouble and playing poorly, I will make an adjustment in the starting line-up for the second half. Sometimes, too, a substitute will be playing so well that I will keep him in the line-up. Over the long NBA season, a superlative performance by a bench player will occasionally provide the difference between a victory and a loss. I am constantly aware of that possibility.

End of Period, End of Game

At the close of a period—and there are four periods in the NBA—the team with the ball will, of course, have the last shot. The final minute of a period is always important, but it is often critical in the fourth period. Because of the NBA's 24-second clock, it is possible to have two good scoring opportunities—compared to one for the opponent—in the last minute. A team in possession of the ball with, for example, 50 seconds remaining will have two 13-second chances to score even if the other team uses the full 24 seconds to get its shot. It's important not to hurry the offense, despite the pressures of the clock. 13 seconds is an adequate time in which to score if play is well organized and executed. A team should know, therefore, exactly what's expected of it in the final minutes, and be able to adapt to whatever offensive or defensive demand the game occasions.

There are only three general circumstances possible as a game nears its end: we're ahead, we're behind, or we're tied. If we're comfortably ahead, I want my team to stay with its normal patterns, looking for a good shot. I don't believe in "garbage time," that aptly named period after a game's outcome has been determined, during which some teams allow their players to accumulate points to fatten their personal averages. I expect my team to always stay in its style of play, whether in practice, a close game, or a runaway. Bad habits, once acquired, have a way of persisting. And in a close game, a bad habit can be costly.

If we have the ball in a game so close that the other team can tie or win on its next possession, I want my team to use as much of the 24 seconds as it can before taking a good shot. In this situation, I have the guards and forwards spread themselves in four-corner positions, while moving the post man between the foul line and the top of the circle, where he can face the ball in any direction. There should then be enough ball movement, passing, and screening away from the ball to both maintain possession and execute a prescribed play within the final ten seconds. Ideally, a set play involving two or three men affords the best shooting opportunity, without jeopardizing defensive transition or the opportunity for an offensive rebound or tip-in. A good play in a critical moment has but one or two passes, though it must allow for options. A guard to center pick and roll, for example, or a weak side forward and guard bump and roll work well in close encounters. Having options takes pressure off the primary player, reinforcing the team's responsibility to make the play work.

Close games also have special defensive requirements which must be studied and practiced in advance. Occasionally I use a surprise defensive tactic against a team with a chance to win on one shot, but my plans rely first on what has been successful before. I will use a double-teaming defense to confuse the other team on rare occasions, though I prefer, as do the players, man-on-man pressure. Sometimes our only opportunity to win lies in gambling to steal an inbounds pass, or double-teaming the first player to get the ball. Whatever is called for, however, must be a part of the team's overall preparation to play.

A final factor to consider in any game is officiating. I've never played or coached in a game won or lost by the referees, but I want to know the kind of game they're likely to call. Some officials allow a lot of contact, others very little. Some will listen to a coach's complaints, other will not. Pointing out the style of officiating they're going to encounter is useful to the players. It won't help them win, but it can't hurt them to know.

After the Game

I always evaluate the game for the players as soon as it's over. My general purpose is to compare the game plan we prepared with the game we actually played, trying to be as objective as I can. I expect the players to stop whatever they're doing, to listen for several minutes and reflect on what we've just done. When I've concluded, they can shower and meet the press, by then aware of my view of the game.

My own obligation to the press, I think, is not unlike that I have to my players in my post-game assessment. I want to be fair and objective in answering their questions, praising when it is deserved and criticizing when necessary. Criticism, however, should be directed at a team's overall play. I never criticize a player in print. It is my job to do that in private, or on occasion before the whole team. Doing it for the press simply undermines trust, and violates my view of the bond between a coach and his players. Criticizing an opposing coach or his team likewise serves no useful purpose. Coaching is a sufficiently competitive and insecure profession as it is, without public quarrels between its members. I try always to emphasize the good things a coach has done or is doing with his team. Red Holzman, when he was coaching the New York Knicks, invariably found something kind to say about his opponent—during the Knicks' championship years he was a gracious winner, just as he avoided unkind remarks during the seasons his aging team finally won less often. He left many friends in the profession when he retired.

I am usually the last person to leave the locker room. Observing the players' reactions to the game helps me prepare for the future. I want to know if a player is more interested in his own play, whether good or bad, than in the team's performance. I want especially to check the attitudes of players who have not played at all, to encourage a player who has had a bad night, to congratulate a player who has played hard, whether in victory or defeat. Spending a few moments with the trainer keeps me informed of injuries. A discussion with my assistant, whose counsel I value, helps complete my overall assessment of the game. Sometimes I watch videotapes of the game, though I just as frequently do that the next morning. By the time I leave, having observed all I can, my perspective on the team and its prospects is enhanced. We'll be better prepared for the next game.

In-Season Progress

The season as a whole should chart a course of constant improvement. Practices based on the continuous evaluation of individual and overall play, the unending preparation for a better performance, help forestall any leveling off in team play. Too many coaches abandon any expectation of real improvement once the season begins. I prefer to look at every game as an opportunity to play at a higher level of competence. Not only can each player work on his own game, but the team can strive for a greater integration of its members. Changes in the players' roles sometimes occur, and that, too, is a product of active, ongoing coaching. A change in the starting line-up, for example, must be introduced and explained with special care. As players gain confidence and poise over the season, their play will show increased consistency. Achieving that consistency is a coach's job.

Comparing films of games played early in the season with those played later demonstrates the process of development. It might, however, indicate a gradual deterioration in some quality of the team's play. In either case, the comparison is instructive. It is similarly profitable to have someone not connected with the team prepare an objective report on its performance. "If you were playing my team," I ask this person, "what kind of scouting report would you make?" Any deviation in what he observes from what I expect points the way to improvement. I must then decide what steps will remedy any weaknesses diagnosed. However well or poorly a team is playing, the coach must remain firmly in control, confident in his style of play.

Off-Season Activity

It's a good idea to put the game aside for a time after the season is over. But while the season's still fresh in my mind, I think about what we've done, whether or not we reached our objectives, where we failed or succeeded. As part of my preparation for the next season, I want to identify the good things we'll want to keep as well as the weaknesses we'll want to eliminate. Doing all this takes time, but my vacation can't begin until it's done.

How do I review a season? I study game films and videotapes. I talk with the players, opposing coaches or anyone else who can give me a knowledgeable and objective appraisal of the season. I spend a lot of time with my assistant, comparing the objectives we planned to achieve at the beginning of the season with what we were able to accomplish. A thorough post-season evaluation is the groundwork for planning summer training programs for the players, providing them with the guidelines they need to work on improving their skills. Talking with each player is a particularly valuable part of this process. I want him to assess for me in detail what he saw as his own contribution to the team. How, I will ask, could he have done more? What did he see as his weaknesses? I also want his opinion on my work. What more could I have done to help him? How, I want him to tell me, might I have contributed more to team development?

On the basis of all of this I give each player a written evaluation of his season's work, including in it the training program he should follow during the off-season. The training programs I prescribe always stress the parts of a player's game in need of improvement. Players tend otherwise to work on their strengths, relying on what they already do well rather than attempting to remedy weaknesses. Most players want to improve, but they can't do it without a clear sense of what it is they need to work on. No player is beyond improvement—not even an NBA star. But simply going to the gym and shooting the ball or playing one-on-one isn't enough. Having a set routine to follow benefits every player, and never more so than when it holds the promise of an improved performance the next season.

I also want the players to maintain their conditioning and flexibility during the off-season. Before every workout, in the summer as during the regular season, the players should

1976-77 N.B.A. CHAMPIONS

trail blazers

July 5, 1977

Dear Maurice:

I just want to congratulate you on the role you played on the World Championship team this past season.

You made great strides in playing within the team concept. Your rebounding and outlet passing from the defensive board, and your improvement on moving without the ball helped us considerably. Your "physical" play was also very important. Areas to improve: offensive board positioning, better defensive positioning and movement, continued improvement in movement without the ball and passing to continue movement.

Next, I want you to set some goals for yourself for the coming season. Initially, you should aim to come to camp in better condition than last year. Secondly, you should be ready to start the season with better skills, referred to earlier. And then, we should all come to camp determined to perform better as a team. That means to execute with the same team purpose but with better movement, better timing and with more efficient play in general. An average cut down of five turnovers a game would be of great benefit. A generally tougher defensive game in which no player permits his man to penetrate will do wonders for the team. The enclosed workout program is similar to the one I sent you last season but with some increases in performance. Follow the program and you will be in the condition necessary for us to win again. The skill drills are to improve your individual game. When you work out, do it with a purpose. These drills will provide the purpose.

Have a good summer. I look forward to seeing you in early September.

Sincerely,

PORTLAND TRAIL BLAZERS

Jack Ramsay
Coach

JR/ss

Portland Trail Blazers • Suite 380 Lloyd Building • 700 NE Multnomah Street • Portland, Oregon 97232 • 503 234-9291

Member National Basketball Association

My letter to Maurice Lucas evaluating his play during the 1976-77 season, including suggestions on how he might prepare during the summer to improve his performance.

portland trail blazers

MEMBER NATIONAL BASKETBALL ASSOCIATION
Phone (503) 234-9291
Suite 380 Lloyd Building • 700 N. E. Multnomah Street • Portland, Oregon 97232

MEMO TO: Portland Trail Blazers Players
FROM: Jack Ramsay
DATE: July 11, 1977
SUBJECT: Summer Training Program

The following program is offered as one to promote (1) steady progression in your general physical conditioning and (2) your personal skills as they relate to an aggressive defensive game and an organized running attack.

Stretchouts should precede <u>and</u> follow each workout. Stretching must be done slowly and followed through to a point of discomfort but not beyond. Daily stretchouts throughout the year are strongly recommended to maintain flexibility and muscle tone.

Maximum times are noted throughout weekly programs. Players should work within their limits but should "push themselves" each workout. Don't feel limited by the suggested maximum times.

Drills suggested for your skill work are those found to have been beneficial in improving game areas of players in the past. Do not limit yourself to these if you have found others to help you more. Do not, however, limit your summer play to half-hearted, half-court play or one-to-one play. Work to improve areas of weakness. Work to maintain areas of strength.

On the first day of training camp (September 23) each player will be required to run a six-minute mile and to complete 300 rope jumps in 2 minutes. Penalties of $1.00 per second over six minutes for the mile run and $1.00 per jump under 300 in two minutes will be imposed on any who cannot meet these standards. These standards have been selected as demonstrating reasonably good fitness for players beginning a professional basketball season. Let each player strive to improve upon his time of last season.

It is vital to the success of our team program that each member attains these basic standards. We do not have the time nor desire to slow down for anyone not in good condition. A quick start in the season depends on your physical readiness.

Be ready!

The summer training program I sent to each member of the Trail Blazers in 1977; it accompanied a personal letter evaluating each player's performance during the 1976-77 season.

portland trail blazers

MEMBER NATIONAL BASKETBALL ASSOCIATION
Phone (503) 234-9291
Suite 380 Lloyd Building • 700 N. E. Multnomah Street • Portland, Oregon 97232

MEMO TO: Portland Trail Blazers Players
FROM: Jack Ramsay
DATE: July 11, 1977
SUBJECT: Stretchouts

ALL STRETCHOUTS MUST BE PERFORMED SLOWLY WITH FULL ROTATION AND STRETCH TOLERANCE.

1. <u>Neck rotation</u>--(3 rotations each direction).

2. <u>Arm rotation</u>--alternate arms (4 turns forward and back).

3. <u>Trunk rotation</u>--hands on hips, feet apart, knees straight, full rotation of trunk (each direction 4 times).

4. <u>Toe touches</u>--feet apart, knees straight, touch outside each foot with hands together (3 times each direction).

5. <u>Stretch out</u>--feet apart, hands on hips, stretch to side bending knee in direction of stretch (alternate side to side 3 times each).

6. <u>Stretch down</u>--feet apart, turn to side and stretch down (3 times each direction).

7. <u>On back leg ups</u>--extend one fully on floor, knee straight, pull other knee to chest, alternate leg pulls (3 times each leg).

8. <u>Knees to chest</u>--on back, shoulders on floor, slowly pull both knees to chest, hold for 10 counts (one time).

9. <u>Hurdle stretch</u>--sit on floor, extend one leg forward, tuck other leg back (assuming approximate hurdle jump position), bring head to extended knee, hold for six seconds (each leg once).

10. <u>Groin squeeze</u>--sitting position, hand palms together, place hands between legs and squeeze using groin muscles, hold for six seconds (one time).

11. <u>Achilles stretch</u>--face wall with feet together about 18 inches away from wall. Keeping feet on floor (heels stay in contact with floor), knees straight, place hands on wall and lean forward until chest reaches wall. Hold for 10 counts. Two repetitions.

portland trail blazers

MEMBER NATIONAL BASKETBALL ASSOCIATION
Phone (503) 234-9291
Suite 380 Lloyd Building • 700 N. E. Multnomah Street • Portland, Oregon 97232

MEMO TO: Portland Trail Blazers Players
FROM: Jack Ramsay
DATE: July 11, 1977
SUBJECT:

July 15-22 (3 days weekly minimum)

1. Stretchouts.
2. Rope jumps (one hundred rope jumps--2 repetitions--maximum time: 1 minute.
3. Quarter mile run (maximum time: 1½ minutes).
4. 50 yard runs (sprint 50-job 50; sprint 50-jog 50--2 repetitions).
5. Quarter mile run (maximum time 1½ minutes).
6. Shooting (personal games shots, free throws--maximum time: 30 minutes).
7. Stretchouts (rope jumps--100 jumps, 2 repetitions--stretch).

July 23-31 (3 days weekly minimum

1. Stretchouts as directed.
2. Rope jumps (100 jumps--maximum time: 1 minute--3 repetitions).
3. Half-mile run (maximum time: 3 minutes).
4. Sprint and jog (sprint 50-jog 50--4 repetitions).
5. Half-mile run (maximum time: 4 minutes).
6. Basketball skill drills (30 minutes).
7. Stretchouts (rope jumps--100 jumps--2 repetitions).

August 1-15 (4 days weekly minimum)

1. Stretchouts.
2. Rope jumps (100 jumps--maximum time: 85 seconds--4 repetitions).
3. Three-quarter mile run (maximum time: 5 minutes)
4. Sprint and jog (sprint 50-jog 50--5 repetitions).
5. Three-quarter mile run (maximum time: 5 minutes).
6. Basketball skill drills (30 minutes).
7. Stretchouts--rope jumps (100 jumps--2 repetitions).

August 15-31 (4 days weekly minimum)

1. Stretchouts.
2. Rope jumps (200 jumps--maximum time: 2 minutes--2 repetitions).
3. Mile run (maximum time: 7 minutes).
4. Sprint and jog (sprint 50-jog 50--5 repetitions).
5. Half-mile run (maximum time: 3 minutes).
6. Skill drills.
7. Stretchouts--rope jumps (100 jumps--2 repetitions).

September 1-15 (5 day weekly minimum)

1. Stretchouts.
2. Rope jumps (300 jumps--maximum time: 2½ minutes--2 repetitions).
3. 2-mile run (maximum time: 14 minutes).
4. Sprint and jog (sprint 50-jog 50--5 repetitions).
5. Skill drills.
6. Stretchouts--rope jumps (100 jumps--2 repetitions).

September 15-22 (5 days weekly minimum)

1. Stretchouts.
2. Rope jumps (300 jumps--maximum time: 2 minutes).
3. 3-mile run (maximum time: 24 minutes) or 1-mile run (maximum time: 6 minutes), alternating days of 3-mile and 1-mile runs.
4. Sprint and jog (sprint 50-jog 50--5 repetitions).
5. Skill drills.
6. Stretchouts--rope jumps (100 jumps--2 repetitions).

stretch before they run. The system of stretching exercises I use was developed by working with Ray Melchiorre, the trainer of the Buffalo Braves, by consulting with Paul Uram, the flexibility coach of the Pittsburgh Steelers, and by studying a manual on stretching by Bob Anderson. The program is designed not only to minimize the likelihood of muscle pulls or sprains, but to increase quickness and muscle power. It requires 15 to 20 minutes a day, and is pleasant as well as beneficial.

As an inspiration to the players to keep fit in the off-season, I expect them on the first day of training camp in the fall to run a mile under six minutes and complete 300 rope jumps in two minutes or less. A modest system of fines is imposed on anyone who fails. Just as with the off-season drills and training programs, the purpose of the Ramsay Mile and the rope-jumping is to give the players a clear objective in their summer conditioning work. A lot of players work especially hard to meet the training requirements, not least because their teammates are sure to ride them if they can't.

Jack Marin, a veteran player acquired by Buffalo from Houston during mid-season when I coached the Braves, had never involved himself in off-season training for basketball. During the summer following his first year at Buffalo, I sent him a letter with some training suggestions, informing him of the six-minute mile requirement. When I greeted Jack at training camp in the fall he laughingly said, "You bastard! You ruined my summer. All I kept thinking about was that mile run. It was screwing up my golf game." But Jack's pride had impelled him to do the extra running. He came to camp in great shape and had a fine season for the Braves. He later admitted that he felt it had been beneficial for him.

There are also several summer professional leagues which provide an opportunity for rookies or young players already in the league who haven't had much playing time to get some experience in professional competition. But as with everything else in the off-season, the playing itself is less important than the chance to work on improving one's skills. The Los Angeles Summer League is the best organized of these leagues. A number of teams send their assistant coaches to work with the young players in the Los Angeles league, providing benefits not only to the players but to the teams as well. Both Jack McKinney and I have spent time there each summer we have been with Portland. Both of us worked with the players at practice and Jack coached the team in the games.

The Los Angeles league benefited the Blazers greatly in 1976. It provided John Davis some of the experience that enabled him to make the transition from college to NBA basketball in a relatively smooth manner. John also had the benefit of practicing there with some of the Blazer personnel like Bob Gross and Lionel Hollins, who were to share starting roles with him in the championship round in the playoffs against Philadelphia in the upcoming season. No one would have anticipated that in the summer of '76.

RAMSAY BASKETBALL

CHAPTER IV

WHAT is this game that runs through my mind? It is a ballet, a graceful sweep and flow of patterned movement, counterpointed by daring and imaginative flights of solitary brilliance. It is a dance which begins with opposition contesting every move. But in the exhilaration of a great performance, the opposition vanishes. The dancer does as he pleases. The game is unified action up and down the floor. It is quickness, it is strength; it is skill, it is stamina; it is five men playing as one. It is tenacity on defense, it is quick penetration on offense. It is taking advantage of every offensive opportunity. It is stifling the opponent, it is jamming up the one on one player. But most of all, it is the spirit of winning as a team. It is the solidarity of a single unifying purpose, the will to overcome adversity, the determination never to give in. It is winning; it is winning; it is winning!

DEFENSE

A team's defense is the foremost part of its overall game plan. Defense dictates tempo, it establishes the flow of a game. Defense triggers the offense. Victory is always within the reach of a strong defensive team. Good defense enables a team to overcome an occasional poor shooting night. A strong defensive team can come from behind to win. A team's personality is established through its defense. Defense, in a word, is dominant.

Individual Defense

Good team defense requires a fundamentally sound defensive contribution from each player. Guards, forwards and centers must all be capable of denying their opponent the open shot or penetration to the basket. A team should be able to win the majority of its games on just these two defensive qualities. It must, in addition, be able to maintain good rebounding position. Imagine a team which denies its opponent any opportunity to penetrate into the scoring area, which contests every shot, and which controls the rebounds after any shots an opponent does manage to take. A team like this would be difficult to beat on the basis of its defensive strength alone. And this would be true regardless of its size, its shooting ability or offensive style. What does it take to play this kind of defense?

All good defensive players are naturally quick, but their effectiveness comes from combining proper technique with their physical gifts. Good defensive technique begins with the correct stance. The defensive player's goal is to keep himself positioned between his opponent and the space that opponent wishes to occupy. In the basic defensive stance, the player keeps his weight slightly forward, on the balls of his feet, with his knees flexed, his head up and his butt down. The body weight is well centered, providing the balance essential to moving rapidly in any direction. The feet and hands are in the same position relative to each other: right hand extended, right foot forward; left hand extended, left foot forward.

Working from the basic stance, each player can begin to fulfill his general defensive responsibilities. He wants, first of all, to keep his opponent who has the ball from penetrating within easy shooting range of the basket. Next he must deny his opponent who wants the ball access to it by contesting every pass, constantly pressuring players trying to get into position to receive a pass. This is a particularly demanding part of pressure defense, requiring an awareness not only of the position of the man being guarded but also of the position of the ball on the

Lionel Hollins has good defensive position as he concentrates on Randy Smith. As Smith drives...

...Hollins moves with him, maintaining his defensive position.

John Davis denies Jo Jo White an opportunity to penetrate.

Hollins and Corky Calhoun pressure their opponents trying to get into position to receive a pass.

court. If the opponent does receive the ball, he shouldn't be allowed to take an open shot. Every shot should be challenged. Each player must be forced to his weakness rather than his strength. Finally, each player should be able to establish a strong defensive rebounding position, staying between his opponent and the basket. The combination of these four ingredients—denying access to easy passes, shutting off the open shot, preventing penetration to the basket, and maintaining strong rebounding position—distinguishes every good defensive player. And winning basketball games begins with good defense, with an aggressive, unyielding opposition by each player to any offensive threat by his opponent.

Walton pressures the passer as Hollins works to deny his man the ball.

As Walton contests the shot, his teammates block out under the basket.

The near defender, Dave Twardzik (#13), moves over to help pressure the shooter.

The Blazers are in ideal rebounding position; the big men are blocking out on the boards, the guards are ready for an outlet pass to start the fastbreak.

Team Defense

No matter how diligently a player pursues his individual defensive objectives, he can only be as effective as the overall quality of his team's defensive play allows. The general objective of team defense is to take an opponent out of his offensive game plan and force it to play a secondary, less effective game. A well-played defense will lead to pass deflections and interceptions, to strong rebounding position, and to a poor shooting percentage by an opponent forced out of its offensive patterns. I want my team to carry the defense to its opponents, to play aggressively but with coordination among its members. If one player gives an advantage by, for example, going for a steal, I want someone there to pick up the open man. The other players should then rotate into position to deny any easy opportunities to score. I want my players always conscious of the fact that, just as they win or lose as a team, they play defense together. A momentary failure by one player increases rather than diminishes the responsibility of his teammates. The team as a whole gives up points, not individual players. Team defense, in which each player has both specific and general responsibilities, is the guiding idea.

I like my players to set up the first line of defense in the midcourt area. The object, as with all defensive alignments, is to force the ball away from the position on the court preferred by the offense. Applying midcourt rather than fullcourt pressure reduces the risk of long scoring passes to players who have got behind the defense. I want my players to automatically pick up at halfcourt whenever the other team gets the ball. Variations of this strategy, such as those we employed in the 1976 playoffs, may be necessary on occasion. In general, however, I set up the first rigid line of defense at midcourt.

The guards have the job of preventing the initial penetration of the ball. Defensive cooperation between the guards is especially important. The guard defending the player with the ball should force him toward the off-guard—toward, this is, the guard without the ball. The best way to do this is to force

Davis hustles to shut off the sideline while Hollins considers double teaming the dribbler.

Davis picks up his man in the backcourt; Hollins keeps between his man and the ball, getting in position to execute a run and jump switch.

Hollins directs Charlie Scott toward the middle, then...

...maintains strong defensive position as Scott tries to move to the sideline. Meanwhile...

...Dave Twardzik moves into position to shut off a pass to White (#10).

the dribbler toward the middle. We can then use either a jump-switch or run and jump switching to forestall the movement of the ball from the back court to the front court. A jump switch is a quick movement by the off-guard defender into the path of the ball-handling guard. In the run and jump switch, the second guard moves diagonally to challenge the man with the ball, while the first guard stays in the passing lane as he moves across the court to pick up the off-guard. Pressure defense by the guards out high will minimize any chances for good scoring opportunities off of a quick penetrating move. Forcing the ball to the middle is effective in inhibiting the guard-to-forward pass with which many teams begin their offensive patterns.

John Davis is about to execute a run and jump switch; Hollins will pick up Davis' man (#12).

Hollins leaves his man to intercept the dribbler as Twardzik moves into position to cut off a pass.

As Davis pressures the ball, his teammates move to deny their men the ball. When his man stops the dribble....

... Davis moves off him. Lucas (#20) fights to keep his man from posting low, as Walton moves over to help out. ...

...Lucas goes up against the shot as Walton blocks out under the basket.

The forwards' defensive responsibility begins with their contesting the guard-to-forward pass. The ball side defensive forward must overplay his man, making it difficult for him to receive a pass. The guards continue their pressing, switching defense on the ballhandler, keeping the offense out of its pattern. The responsibilities of the other two defenders—the off-side forward and the center—are dictated in part by the ability of the other three defenders to carry out their assignments. The off-side forward and the center want to keep their men from receiving an easy pass, particularly in a position where they can relay it to a teammate cutting toward the basket. They must also be prepared to leave their man if an opponent who is being overplayed makes a quick cut to the basket. They will be ready to overplay against a pass if the ball is reversed from one side of the court to the other.

Lloyd Neal (#36) overplays the ball side forward to prevent an easy pass.

Good team defense makes it hard for the passer to find anyone open.

Well played team defense is beautiful to watch. It involves pressure on the man with the ball, switching, overplaying, and always, always, helping out. A player will leave his man to block an opponent's shot, knowing that a teammate will pick up the man he left. He will go for a steal, which is often the beginning of a fastbreak opportunity, with the same assurance. Team defense can also keep an offensive player from posting up, denying an opponent yet another aspect of its offensive game. A player posts-up by standing six to ten feet from the basket with his back turned to it ready to receive a pass for a turning jump shot. It's imperative to keep that player from getting the ball. One defender must move in front of him to deny the pass, while the weak side defender moves between him and the basket. In this situation, all the defenders must rotate to cover any player open to receive a pass. Again, everyone helps out.

As the other defenders overplay their men, Davis forces the dribbler toward the middle, where Hollins waits to cut him off.

As Larry Steele moves his man into the middle, Davis moves toward the dribbler; Bill Walton is in position to cut off any move into the lane.

From Defense to Offense

Sound, aggressive defense is the foundation upon which a winning basketball team rests. Tough defense means diving for loose balls, taking the charge from a player driving to the basket, and chasing down an opponent going in for a "sure layup." Not least of all, good defense creates scoring opportunities, whether from steals, interceptions, or through maintaining good rebounding position. A fastbreak offense goes hand-in-hand with an aggressive defense. I like turning an opponent's errors into quick scores. Besides, if our offense begins only after we've taken the ball out of the net following the other team's basket, we're not going to win very many ball games.

Twardzik and Gross, defending on the weakside (away from the ball), are ready to pick off any pass thrown into the lane.

Communication is essential to good defense. Bill Walton directs his teammates as they move to recover against a fastbreak.

Success in the fastbreak game I coach requires good rebounding, sharp outlet passing, deft ball handling, quick lane filling, accurate shooting, and great speed in getting down the floor. It's a fun way to play and an interesting style to watch. Most teams will fastbreak if the chance arises, but we're always looking to run. The traditional fastbreak develops when one man gets behind the defense for a long pass, or in a quick movement down the floor with the offensive players outnumbering the defenders, usually two on one or three on two. We look for this kind of break, practicing the good outlet passes, ball handling and running to fill the lanes which it requires. My ideas on the execution of the traditional fastbreak differ little from those of any other coach. I depart from standard fastbreak theory, however, in continuing the offensive attack without bringing the ball back outside for a set offensive series if a basket doesn't materialize on the break itself.

In every running situation we want to get the ball to the ballhandler with a quick outlet pass, fill the lanes with players who will cut sharply to the basket ready to receive a pass, and move the ball up court as quickly as possible. Our purpose is to get the ball into our offensive zone before the defense sets up, whether after a missed shot or a score. The ballhandler in the middle is particularly important in controlling the flow of the game and sustaining the pace of the attack. One player of the five on the floor should have this responsibility. We want the best ballhandler to run the break, keeping the whole court within his vision as he looks for teammates in position behind the defense to receive a pass. But the team as a whole makes the fastbreak work, exploiting every opportunity for a quick basket. Every player must be in top condition for the team to execute its running game.

I use a simple but effective drill in practice everyday to sharpen our execution of the basic movements of the three on two or two on one fastbreak. The drill begins with three offensive players under one basket and two defensive men in the opposite halfcourt. A ballhandler in the middle, and two wingmen running slightly ahead of the ballhandler near the

As Walton grabs the defensive rebound, he looks for the outlet man while still in the air.

The key to the fastbreak offense is quick transition; everyone's off and running as Walton hits Hollins with the outlet pass.

Lucas blocks a shot by the Bullets' Elvin Hayes; Walton is in position to complete a good defensive play by recovering the ball.

The Blazers are in perfect position on the fastbreak; Davis is about to hit Lucas for the layup.

Lucas rebounds in position to trigger the break; the big forward as well as the center has to throw the outlet pass.

Walton hits Twardzik with the ball as Hollins and Gross fill the lanes on either side of the court.

Everyone has to be ready to run on the break; here Walton fills a lane as Lucas throws the outlet pass.

The small forward has to run, rebound and shoot in the fastbreak offense; Bob Gross takes a rebound...

... and then trails the break as Lucas and Walton break out to fill the lanes.

A relentless pace to beat the opponent down the floor creates the fastbreak advantage.

The defense matches the offense, the signal for the beginning of the turnout pattern; Twardzik, the ballhandler, will establish the ball side of the court.

sidelines, try to score against the two defensive men, who try in turn to stop the break however they can. The player who shoots the ball must then retreat on defense, while the two players who had been on defense fastbreak toward the other basket. The action in this drill is continuous. The two players remaining from the original three on one offense move to defense as the next group of three attacking players brings the ball up court.

Whenever we have an opportunity to run the fastbreak, I want to press our advantage even if the opponent has three defenders back against the three-man break. The fourth and fifth players get into the scoring zone as quickly as possible, joining their teammates before the defense has a chance to get organized. Continuous motion by the offense keeps the defense off balance, even if it has been able to stop our initial offensive surge. Persistence in maintaining a relentless attack often produces easy field goals. We don't want to relinquish the advantages the fast break provides by slowing down our offense.

The reserves carry out the game plan; all the starters are on the bench as Neal rebounds...

...throws the outlet pass to Davis, while Owens, Calhoun and Steele fill the lanes. When he gets the ball, Davis...

The Turnout

Success in a three-on-two or two-on-one fastbreak is largely a matter of good execution. The key to a fastbreak offense, however, is the use of continous motion after the defense has recovered its position. Even in the most relentless running attack, the offense manages to outnumber the defense in the attacking zone only about ten percent of the time. During the remainder of the time, when the number of defenders equals the number of offensive players, how does the offense keep itself on the attack? The most effective maneuver for staying in motion off of the initial three-on-three offensive thrust is a technique I call the turnout.

There are three basic court positions in the turnout: that of the ballhandler, whose side of the court is called the "ball side;" the wingman on the ball side; and the wingman on the "weak side," or the side away from the ball. The wingman on

...moves to the middle as the ballhandler. Calhoun and Owens move to initiate the turnout; Steele is the trailer.

Hollins takes a long rebound, sees that Gross has an open court before him....

...Hollins hits Gross with a long pass, and . . .

...Gross goes in for the easy score.

the ball side sets a screen near the baseline for the wingman crossing under the basket from the weak side. If the screen is effective, the weak side wingman will be free to take a quick pass from the ballhandler for an easy jump shot. If the defensive men don't switch well, the ball side forward may get free for a pass under the basket. Anytime the defense matches up in a three-on-three situation, we automatically run the turnout. If the turnout doesn't lead to a score, the motion continues as the other two players, usually the center and the big forward, join in the offense.

The positions in the motion offense are relatively fixed. Every position has an important role in the offense, but the key to the success of the turnout offense is the play of the ballhandler and the postman. The ballhandler screens down toward the baseline after making his initial pass to the weak side wingman. The ball side wingman cuts off the screen to move into position at the top of the circle. The center, or postman, takes a low post position on the ball side, while the

The Blazers execute the turnout; Calhoun (#10), the weak side wingman, crosses under the basket to use Walton's screen.

Hollins uses Gross' screen on the turnout as Walton posts up.

Larry Steele cuts off Neal's screen on the turnout as Owens (in the lane) fights past Dave Cowens to get to the post position.

fifth man down goes to the weak side baseline near the lane. All five players are now in their basic positions for the motion offense. The "turnout man"—the wingman who received the first pass from the ballhandler—has three options. The first, as I've mentioned, is to shoot if he's open. He may also pass to the postman, and then split off the post with the player at the

Bob Gross gets free for the baseline jumper from a turnout screen.

Calhoun (on the left side of the picture) passes to Neal at the top of the circle, then...

...Calhoun rubs his man off a Walton screen, but...

...Corky does not get open, so Neal passes to Walton in the medium post as Steele and Twardzik (on the right side of the picture) get ready to cut through the lane.

Gross has passed to Walton, screened for Lucas, and then cut to the basket, where...

...he is in position to take Walton's quick pass for a layup.

top of the circle, rub his man off a pick by the postman, and take a return pass for an open shot in the lane. If he does not get the return pass, he goes on across the lane to screen for the fifth man down the floor, who is on the weak side baseline position. The player at the top of the circle then passes the ball back to the postman, who has three options. He looks first for the player cutting from the weak side baseline off the screen by the turnout man. His second option is a pass to the ball-handler, who has circled back to become the second cutter through the lane. If neither of these passes is available, he will look for the turnout man coming back into the foul lane area off a screen set by the player who made the pass to the postman. There are seven quick scoring opportunities in this sequence, ranging from layups to jump shots from a maximum distance of eighteen feet.

Walton looks for the open man on a split off the post; everyone but Walton is in motion.

Gross rubs off, gets free under the basket as Neal passes to Owens; Davis, on the opposite side of the court from Owens, prepares to cut baseline off the screen Gross will set on the weak side.

Davis, the baseline cutter, is about to get a pass from Walton under the basket.

Walton hits Twardzik cutting through the lane as he looks away from his receiver, then....

...Dave reverses a spinner off the glass for two.

Hollins, as the baseline cutter, has received a pass from Walton after moving off a Lucas screen; if Bill had not passed to Lionel then Lucas, the original rub-off cutter, would have curled back into the lane for a jumper.

Even if it fails to produce a basket, the turnout offense leads easily into the passing game. Like the turnout, the passing game is designed for continuous motion leading to a good shot. The passing game is developed off the postman's pass to the weak side baseline player, who has moved back into the lane for the pass and an opportunity to shoot. Following his pass, the postman screens down for the baseline cutter, who comes back through the lane on his cut. The ballhandler will then step off the postman's screen to take a pass within good range for a jump shot. In the passing game, any player making a pass screens down toward the baseline for two other players, the first of whom cuts through the lane, while the other steps out along the foul lane, in position for a jump shot. Either of these players should be in good position to take a pass. If the defense is overplaying in an attempt to cut off the pass, players have the option of cutting backdoor or screening back down for a player on the baseline. The passing game provides high percentage shots as well as good ball and player movement.

When the turnout man is unable to get the ball, the ballhandler can initiate any one of several options. If the turnout man is unable to get the ball because of an overplaying defense, the ballhandler can delay momentarily as the postman takes up his position ready to receive the ball. A pass to the postman then signals the beginning of a backdoor series. The turnout man makes a backdoor cut, the ballhandler cuts into the lane, and the ball side wingman splits off the postman

Lloyd Neal, the rub-off cutter, curls back into the middle for an open jumper.

Walton hits Calhoun going backdoor; Bill's technique of passing when close to his defender makes the play effective.

from the top of the circle. The success of the backdoor series depends on the ability of the postman to see the open man, particularly the backdoor cutter, and get the ball to him in traffic. Backdoor opportunities are created by the defense's attempt to shut off the initial pass to the turnout man.

The ballhandler has a second option if neither the turnout man nor the postman is in a good position to receive a pass. The ball side wingman can flash to the high post for a pass from the ballhandler. He can then make a backdoor pass to the last man up the floor or, if the defense is set, to the weak side guard. The passing guard or ballhandler follows his pass on this option, so that if the backdoor cutter isn't open, a two-man situation sets itself up for the flash pass receiver and the passing guard. The backdoor cutter continues his arc under the basket, coming around a double screen set by the postman and a turnout cutter, in position to receive a pass for a short jump shot.

If the turnout man, the postman and the flashman are all covered, the ballhandler can simply reverse the ball to the other guard for a pass to the weak side forward, starting another turnout series on the opposite side of the floor. The advantages of this offense are numerous. A running, quick breaking, penetrating attack executed with speed, quickness and good ball handling guarantees easy baskets against an opponent which is slow in making the transition from offense to defense. But even against a defense which does recover and match up well, it provides high percentage shots. It is an offense which runs smoothly and quickly without the necessity of slowing down play to set up a pattern. It is a continuous motion rather than a set up offense. Finally, it has the advantage of keeping every player in the offense. It erases any doubt in a player's mind about what his responsibilities are, as every player must work to keep the offense in motion. He doesn't have to think about what play is being run, or whether the break is on. In this attack, the break is always on—even five-on-five is a breaking situation.

Additional Options in the Turnout Attack

There are several basic options in the turnout attack, all designed to take advantage of the defensive lapses which an attacking style of play will generate. The ballhandler always has the option of driving to the basket when there is an opening in the lane. He can then score a layup or, if he draws a defender away from his man, pass off to an open teammate. Any player handling the ball should look for teammates going backdoor. In addition, the ball side wingman must always look for mismatches or over-adjustments. If two defenders go out to cover the turnout man, the screening wingman can take the open shot under the basket off of a quick pass. If the defender on the ball side wingman is smaller than the man he's guarding, the wingman can post the shorter man down deep. The postman will also have frequent opportunities to go backdoor for a pass from the turnout man. This is especially likely to occur when the defender overplays against the pass as the postman moves from the weak side across the lane. By making a quick move toward the lane before cutting to the basket, the postman can free himself for a high lob pass under the basket.

When the three-man turnout is in progress, the fourth and fifth men down the floor—the "trailers"—will often find themselves open. The fourth man in particular can free himself for a layup by quickly changing direction on a movement through the lane. If the defender sags into the middle to counteract this move through the lane, the trailer can pull up for an open fifteen-foot jumper from the weak side. These basketball plays are a natural product of the quick action generated by the turnout offense.

Set Options

A number of set options, most originating in a quick cut to the ball side baseline by the ballhandler following a pass to the turnout man, keep variety in the attack. These options are keyed by a verbal or visual signal. The raised clinched fist, for

Gross hits Walton with a lob pass under the basket; Bill cut back when his defender tried to keep him from moving into his post position on the ball side.

Walton and Gross, raising their clenched fists, signal the beginning of the down series.

In the down series, Lucas has passed to Gross and cut through the lane, and Twardzik has cut to the baseline to get free for an open shot off a Walton screen.

example, indicates the beginning of the "down series." In this series, the postman is at the medium post position, the ball side wingman is at the top of the circle, and the weak side guard is opposite the turnout man. If the ball is reversed to the top of the circle, the players on the ball side can set screens for the turnout man. The turnout man can also set a double screen with the postman, creating an option for the guard on the baseline to pop out for a short jumper over the screens, or to cut baseline for a pass from the weak side wingman. The postman has the option of rolling quickly into the lane for a pass from the top of the circle.

The postman can also set up in the high post, looking for back door cuts by the weak side guard or posting low by the deep forward. In these options, as with all movement in the turnout attack, the key to good execution is quick passing and coordinated movement. In order for the timing to be precise, no player should hold the ball for more than a two-second count.

Twardzik has just taken a pass from Gross in the down series option, as Hollins and Walton screen for Lucas, who...

...cuts open in the lane for a pass from Twardzik and...

...an easy layup for Lucas. Hollins is also open curling back into the lane.

John Davis sets his man up for a baseline cut in the down series. Neal is in position to pass to the weak side.

Gross has cut through the lane but is not open, so Walton passes below his defender's outstretched arms to Lucas, who has his man posted deep.

Walton is in position for the high post option, as Gross prepares to pop out for a jumper off Bill's screen; if he can't get open, Gross will clear out so that Twardzik (#13 with the ball) can run a pick and roll with Walton.

Competition

Nothing counts more in the success of the turnout offense than a relentless pace. Every player on the team is essential to the maintenance of constantly pressing, perpetually attacking tempo. As starting players tire, the bench provides the infusion of energy needed to keep up the overall level of speed required by the game plan. Knowing that every player will contribute reinforces the unselfish, team-oriented tendencies of the turnout game itself. A tiring player relinquishes his role to a fresh player, aware that a decrease in pace by anyone will inhibit the play of the whole team.

The ultimate test for any team comes in competition. A truly sound, well-rehearsed game plan, carried out by players confident in their own and their teammates' abilities, will withstand the pressures of the fiercest competition. And when it does, I see on the floor the game that runs through my mind. I see an unsuspecting opponent lured into an untenable defensive position, caught in the steel trap snap of the execution. I see a defender suddenly appear, like a sixth man on the floor, to disrupt an unwary opponent's well-planned scoring play. I see an endless stream of defenders so thoroughly thwarting an offensive attempt that only the buzzing of the 24-second clock relieves the opponent's misery. Finally, I see my team's relentless attack and zealous defense exhaust our opponent, leading us to victory. I like what I see; I could watch it forever.

PLAYING IN THE NBA

CHAPTER V

BASKETBALL has come a long way from the Eastern YMCAs and recreation halls where it first took hold barely 80 years ago. International amateur play, as the quality of the Olympic tournament attests, is improving rapidly. European professional leagues are attracting thousands of fans, drawn by the popularity of the game and the many good American players now on European teams. But the best basketball in the world, the most intensely competitive of all, is played in the NBA. The players are bigger, quicker, better conditioned and more highly skilled than players anywhere else. Every NBA team is good, though some are clearly better than others. But a very fine line separates the best teams in the League from the worst; there are no "bad" players on any team. There are, after all, only about 250 players in the NBA at any time, a tiny number compared to the hundreds of thousands of players who learn the game. The talent in the League is highly concentrated. Winning in the NBA is never easy; capturing a League Championship is the greatest challenge in basketball.

Consistency at home and on the road—and from season to season—is the hallmark of a great team. But the overall quality of the players makes it especially difficult for one team to win year after year in the NBA. Not since the Boston Celtics won consecutive titles in 1968-69 has a team successfully defended a League title. Maintaining a competitive edge is a delicate matter. An injury to a key player, for example, particularly during the playoffs, can mean the difference between winning and losing. Making poor draft choices will obviously weaken a team in the long run. In addition, the quality of officiating, the skills of a team's management and the problems associated with the long NBA schedule all influence the way the game is played. A coach must be aware of every factor, however subtle, that affects his team. There's more to playing in the NBA than meets the eye.

The League Structure

The National Basketball Association was formally created in 1949 by a merger between two rival leagues, the Basketball Association of America and the National League. Its original organizers were primarily owners of hockey arenas looking for some attraction to fill their buildings on the open dates created by the hockey teams' road trips. College basketball was then immensely popular, suggesting to the organizers of professional basketball a natural audience on which to draw. The response, unfortunately, was not what they had expected; the fans stayed away in droves. The quality of play was good, but even the best teams had difficulty surviving. The early history of the League was littered with vagabond franchises looking for a place to settle. Something had to be done to distinguish the pro game, to bring its rules into conformity with the talents of its players. The playoffs had stimulated interest from the beginning, but a few packed houses at the end of the year couldn't recoup the losses accumulated during the season. The future of the NBA looked unpromising in the early fifties. But in 1954, with the adoption of a 24-seconds-to-shoot rule, the NBA discovered the means of its salvation. The 24-second rule was the single greatest innovation in the development of professional basketball. It was suggested by Danny Biasone, the owner of the Syracuse Nats, who realized that without a rule requiring a team to shoot within a certain time after acquiring possession of the ball, teams could sit on a lead, freezing the action with stalling tactics. The results were predictably boring; the best players in the world, rather than putting their skills on display, often stood holding the ball. But with the installation of a 24-second clock, a team had to shoot or lose the ball. Professional basketball was immediately transformed. Good defensive play was as important as ever, but team scoring averages throughout the League rose dramatically. There were more close games, more exciting finishes. The NBA's real history began in 1954, accompanied by a steady rise in the League's popularity.

In 1976, the NBA absorbed four teams from the American Basketball Association, creating its current 22-team structure. The League is now divided into four roughly geographical Divisions—the Pacific, Midwest, Atlantic and Central—and two Conferences, the Eastern and the Western. The NBA is headed by a Commissioner—Lawrence O'Brien now occupies the post—who is appointed by and acts for its Board of Governors. The Board, consisting of the team owners and their representatives, establishes the rules and regulations governing play; the Commissioner's office carries them out. The Commissioner has the authority to suspend a player, to approve player trades, and to levy fines of up to 25 thousand dollars against players, coaches, front office staff or even team owners who violate League rules. A technical foul, for example, is an automatic seventy-five dollar fine payable to the League office. A particularly irate player or coach can take advantage of the Commissioner's Special: two technical fouls and ejection from the game for only two hundred and twenty-five bucks. I have, on rare occasions, contributed to the League's coffers; the team, however, typically pays a coach's fines.

Beyond its policing duties the Commissioner's office has other important responsibilities, among them designing the playing schedule, hiring and training officials, and administering the annual draft of college players. Each of these functions is, in the long run, an important factor in an NBA team's success. The League's obligation is simply to insure that the schedule doesn't favor one team over another, that officiating is competent and impartial, and that the draft provides an opportunity for an equitable distribution of new player talent throughout the League. Each team's management, however, is responsible for protecting its team's interest. The schedule, for example, is based on the availability of the arenas in which the teams play. Each team sends the League a list of approximately 55 dates during which its arena will be available, hoping particularly to schedule games on weekends. Every team's regular season schedule is then evenly divided between home and away games. Most teams play each other four times; against two opponents, however, there will be three games scheduled rather than four, making a total of 82 games. The number of games is specified in the agreement between the League and the Players' Association. No team has an advantage in the number of games it plays; some teams, however, have more difficult road trips than others. A careful look at the schedule will indicate how factors as subtle as the preparation for and arrangement of road trips can make one team's season slightly less burdensome than another's. And in the NBA, the margin between winning and losing is always narrow.

Home and Away. The NBA Schedule

It's a well-known fact of NBA life that few teams lose regularly at home, while an equally small number win consistently on the road. In the 1976-77 season, not a single NBA team won more games than it lost on the road. That disparity proves, perhaps better than anything else can, how slight the gap is which separates the good teams in the League from the poor ones. The skills of the players and the ability of both players and coaches to do their jobs well wherever they are playing are the really critical factors dividing winners from losers. The home court advantage and the hazards of the road are real nonetheless. The benefits of playing at home are easy to pinpoint: the court is familiar, the fans encourage the team, the players are living at home, eating and sleeping regularly—everything is routine. And the opponent, of course, is playing away from home. On the road, however, the dangers are many and the pleasures are few.

Most teams make long road trips when, for example, a circus or an ice show is scheduled in their home arena. Since every team plays most other teams twice, there will be at least two long swings across the country during the regular season. A sensitive and responsible management can help its team win on the road by arranging several short trips rather than a single long journey. Although the League office plans the overall schedule, it's possible for a team to have an influence on the number of games it will play on a *given* road trip. A simple maxim applies here: the longer the road trip, the greater the difficulty in winning. Exhaustion accumulates, so the last games of a road trip are the hardest. The best schedule avoids both overlong road trips and lengthy lay-offs. Ideally, the team should have a day of rest between games; if that's not possible, it should never play on more than two consecutive nights. The probability of losing on the road is always high, but it is even greater if a road trip lasts more than four games over seven or eight days. I work closely with the team trainer, who is the traveling secretary on NBA teams, to design the best possible timetable for our road trips within the limits of the League schedule. I prefer to arrive where we're going to play at least a day before the game, using the day off to overcome jet lag, to practice and to rest. If we're playing Philadelphia on Tuesday, for example, I would want to leave Portland on Sunday. If that means paying for an extra day's hotel rooms and meals, then the team management will have to budget the extra costs. In the long run, the revenue generated by a winning team should more than offset the expense involved in planning an accommodating schedule.

The best schedule in the world, however, is still no guarantee that a team will win on the road. In 1976-77, during the best season in the team's history, the Trail Blazers won only 14 of their 41 games on the road; even with that small total of victories, it set a team record for road wins. At the same time, the Blazers won 35 home games, losing only six. During the playoffs, however, the Blazers were undefeated at home while winning 4 out of 9 games on the road. But road trips are never longer than two games in the playoffs, thereby minimizing the effect of travel on the quality of play.

Physical exhaustion isn't the only hazard a team faces on a long trip. Because it's so difficult for the players to avail themselves of the normal diversions other travelers enjoy, they spend a lot of time in one another's company hanging around their hotel rooms. If there is friction among the players or coaches, the stresses of the road will magnify it. Winning alleviates the strain better than any coach's nostrum, but when losses accumulate and the mood is darkening, the coach has to apply a soothing balm. Preparing the players for the inevitable pressures of the close confinement on the road is an essential part of coaching in the NBA. A team on the road is like a family, dependent on its members for the comforts and pleasures of everyday life. The players share a special intimacy in the powerful emotional moments bred by a crucial victory or a telling loss. There is nothing more exhilirating than a great win and nothing more crushing than a critical loss. The true character of a team—and of a coach—emerges under the stress of crucial games, whether won or lost; feelings can't be hidden or disguised. A coach who knows himself well, whose attitudes are familiar to the players, will manage these moments best. Good teams will keep their equilibrium because there is a mutual respect and understanding among the players and coaches, an appreciation that everyone has a job to do. Bill Bradley, when he was playing on the New York Knicks Championship teams, summarized well the essential ingredient in the stability of a good team. "Disagreements," he said, "never reach the point of bitterness."

Learning to stay on an even keel through the buffeting of an NBA season begins in training camp, where players encounter one another under conditions resembling those they'll later face on the road. Unlike some coaches, I always hold training camp beyond commuting distance from the player's homes, usually on a college campus. Beyond providing the time to establish team goals, define player roles and start the process of blending the team's playing skills, the days spent in training camp give players a chance to get to know one another as traveling companions as well as basketball players. Training camp is a rehearsal for the season, the most important period of the team's development. It prepares the players for the rigors of the season as well as in the style of game they will play. Practices at camp are tough, twice a day for two hours each; in them players learn who plays well when he's tired, who has the best endurance, who has the shortest temper or the least developed taste for hard work. They discover whom among their teammates they will want to spend time with off the court and whom they will regard simply as fellow players. It is a time for new players, especially, to find their place on the team.

Professional basketball training camps are, compared to those in other sports, relatively brief. The entire training period, from the beginning of camp to the first regular season game, is limited to one month by an agreement between the League and the Players' Association. Since there are also up to eight exhibition games to play during that month, training camp lasts only a week or so. There's nothing in the NBA to compare to the leisurely spring training of baseball or the long fall camps of professional football. It hasn't always been this way. When I first came into the NBA, teams played from 12 to 17 exhibition games and required their players to report to training camp as early as they liked. There's merit in restricting the length of the training period, but I think six weeks, rather than a month, would be preferable, allowing me as well as the players adequate time to prepare ourselves for the season. But the pace of the seasons vary from sport to sport, so perhaps it is in keeping with the NBA's character that the training camp is abbreviated. Football teams play once a week, giving them plenty of time to prepare for a game; baseball teams always play one another in a series, enabling them to adjust to their opponents; but basketball teams play one game after another against numerous opponents with little time in between. The training period, therefore, gives a taste of what will follow.

On a typical four-game road trip lasting a week or more, the Trail Blazers will cover from six to eight thousand miles, have two or three regular practices and four game-day previews and shooting practices as well as play. They will then still have plenty of dead spots in the schedule during which they try to find something to do to alleviate boredom.

A road trip often begins on Monday, which is usually a travel day in the NBA. We would get to the airport at 7:00 a.m., for example, ready to fly to Houston for a Tuesday game. After arriving, checking into our hotel and resting for a while, we would have a regular two-hour practice, usually at a local college court. On game days, we would practice briefly in the arena where our game was scheduled. Following practice on an off day, there generally isn't much to do. The players can't act like ordinary tourists because they're so easily recognized. Going to a restaurant or movie, which most players like to do, carries the risk of intrusion; it's impossible for someone like Bill or Luke to be unobtrusive. Even if people don't know exactly who the players are, they generally make the correct assumption that a dozen large men travelling together are a basketball team. Sometimes the constant questions—"Who are you?" or "Are you a basketball player?" or "Why didn't you win last night?"—get tiresome. Talking with fans and signing autographs is a part of the life most players willingly accept, but weary and among strangers on a long trip, they may prefer to retreat. So rather than going out, they stay in their hotel rooms reading or watching TV. When they do venture out, a little deception is sometimes their only guarantee of privacy. It occasionally works even for the best known players.

Bill Walton is very accommodating to people who stop him for a word or an autograph. Once, on a trip to New York, Bill must have signed a hundred autographs at the airport and dozens more on the sidewalk outside our hotel. When he finally made his way inside to the lobby, he was startled by the question of a distinguished looking elderly man who suddenly stood before him. "Who are you?" Bill was asked.

Disbelieving what he had heard, Bill responded with the first name that popped into his head. "Sam," Bill replied, "Sam Washington."

"Well," the man resumed, "are you a basketball player?"

"No," Walton deadpanned.

"Oh, I thought you were with this team," continued the old man, indicating with a sweep of his arm the other Trail Blazers gathered in the lobby.

"Nah. I don't know those guys."

"I'm terribly sorry to have disturbed you," said the man as he backed away from Bill, looking inquiringly into the faces of the other players, clearly puzzled by his error. The players managed to keep from laughing until he was well away from the lobby.

Not all fans are so polite; some are even admirably persistent. I remember once having my nap interrupted at our hotel in New York. "Cleaning lady," said a voice from the door.

I thought that was a little odd, but I was a bit groggy with sleep. "Your sons are here to see you," the voice continued.

I knew that one of my sons was in Buffalo and the other in Olympia, Washington, but I answered the door out of curiosity anyway. There were two boys standing there with autograph pads. "Come on coach, give us your autograph. We missed you in the lobby." How could I refuse?

The rare pestering fan is a minor annoyance compared to the tedium of travel. We usually fly to the next city on a road trip the morning after a game, though we occasionally have to go directly to the airport from the arena for a night flight. Leaving Houston, for example, to continue our imaginary four-game trip, we would go to Atlanta. Arriving there at midday, we would follow the same pattern as in Houston: settle at the hotel, have a practice, come back to the hotel to rest for the next day's game. Sometimes we go directly to practice from the airport. When the game is over, the pattern repeats. Sometimes it seems endless: from airport to hotel to arena to airport to hotel.... If it's Friday, this must be Boston.

Officiating

Analyses of the disparity between the home and away records of NBA teams sometimes point an accusing finger at the referees; officiating, they claim, is biased in favor of the home team. I don't think there is any substance to that charge. Officials may sometimes succumb to baiting from the fans, momentarily losing their concentration. Letting the crowds affect them will surely influence their performance, but good referees, like players and coaches, ignore abuse from the stands. NBA basketball is, anyway, impossible to officiate; given that somewhat severe limitation, most referees work hard to do a good job. The players are so big and fast, the pace of the game so intense, that no one can control—or even see—everything that happens. The best officials try to follow the action away from the ball, but the tendency of referees, like everyone else, is to focus their attention on scoring plays.

Both the importance and the difficulty of officiating in the NBA are, I think, underestimated. Just as with a good team, a referee's greatest virtue is consistency: calling the same play in the same way against both teams regardless of the stage of a game or its importance. A referee who allows loose play early in a game, for example, may find himself unable to assert control later on. Conversely, an official too anxious to establish his authority may never let a game develop its natural momentum. Competent referees have an easy authority, a rapport with players and coaches, a capacity to keep a steady presence in the most demanding circumstances, and a sturdy understanding of the game. They have to be in good shape, they have to be intelligent, they must have acute powers of observation. There are, needless to say, few perfect specimens of the breed.

In the early days of the NBA, coaches consciously intimidated referees, trading a technical foul once in a while for a chance to influence the officiating. Red Auerbach, when he was coaching the Boston Celtics, made a fine art of referee baiting. It's still important to talk to officials, to point out violations they may be missing, but it's no longer common for NBA coaches to harass referees as a matter of policy. It is even necessary at times to take a technical foul to make a point, but antagonizing the referees can have unhappy consequences. Avoiding two technicals and ejection from the game is especially important; it's hard to coach when you can't see the game. When I first started coaching the 76ers, referee Norm Drucker threw me out of a game which we were losing badly to the New York Knicks. Heading for the locker room I told the Sixer's guard, Hal Greer, to have the team press the Knicks after every score we made. After I had been in the locker room a few minutes, I heard the noise from the crowd steadily increasing in volume; I couldn't resist sticking my head out to see if I could learn what was happening. The press was working, I found, and the Sixers were coming back. I started moving closer, edging my way up the tunnel from the locker room to the playing floor. Before long I had wormed my way through a crowd of arena employees to a place just behind a row of security guards stationed at the entrance to the tunnel; from there I watched an ultimately futile Philadelphia rally.

The next day I got a call from Walter Kennedy, who was then the League Commissioner. "Jack," he asked me, "do you know what you're supposed to do when the referee throws you out of the game?"

I told him that I did know. "Well," he continued, "did you come out of the locker room yesterday?"

"I came out into the tunnel," I admitted.

"I thought you did," Kennedy said. "In fact, there's a nice picture of you in the paper today watching the game." What could I say? I was just glad I hadn't tried to deny coming out in the first place. I did regret, however, having to pay a $100 fine for not staying in the locker room.

I learned then, though it was a lesson I had to repeat, that letting my distress with the referees get the best of me only harmed my team's chances of winning. When I was coaching at Buffalo, we were playing Los Angeles in the first game of our first West Coast road trip. The team was in a slump after having started well, and I was feeling the frustrations of losing. We started off poorly against the Lakers; I didn't think the referees, Darrell Garretson and Jimmy Clark, were giving us the calls we deserved. On a fastbreak attempt near our bench, the Lakers' Gail Goodrich grabbed Buffalo's Randy Smith as he drove to the basket. No foul was called; Smith's shot missed badly, the Lakers rebounded and headed up the floor. I jumped from my squatting position by the bench to yell at Clark for missing the foul. Garretson, watching the play from the far end of the court, charged me with a technical. The Lakers scored on the free throw awarded for the technical. As the teams came back up the floor, I called out to Clark. "Jimmy, why didn't you make the call?"

"There wasn't any call to make," he replied as he passed the bench.

I had a great come-back for that. "Yeah, well, you didn't even have the balls to call the technical; Garretson had to make it."

Clark demonstrated that he was, in fact, fully equipped by hitting me with a second technical and tossing me out of the game. And we were still in the first quarter. I was sitting morosely in the locker room as the team came in at halftime. We were, I learned, behind by 19; we finally lost by 27. We might have lost anyway, but it was my job to coach and I wasn't there to do it. My crack at Jimmy Clark may have cost us a ball game. I was out of line abusing him, even if I did feel justified in disputing his judgment. He missed a call, but he wasn't out to get me; I forced him to whistle the technical. There have been times, however, when the referees just seem to be waiting for any excuse to call the Tee.

Some years ago, when I was with Philadelphia, the Sixers had a Sunday afternoon road game scheduled with the Washington Bullets. It's tough to get ready for a 1:30 starting time; the Sixers started the game playing as if they were still asleep. We fell behind by 20 points in the first quarter. As the game went on, the Sixers slowly roused themselves, closing to within two points with a minute left to play. Then Luke

Jackson of the Sixers rammed home an offensive rebound as the referee's whistle sounded. I thought he had been fouled on the play, giving us a chance to go ahead on a free throw. But the official, Jack Madden, called Jackson for walking instead—the basket didn't count. I was stunned. I collapsed on my chair in dismay. Then my chair collapsed under me; it folded as I fell on my back. Madden looked over at me, observing the evidence: I was lying flat on my back, the chair was pushed out on the edge of the court. He assumed, I guess, that I had thrown the chair and was reclining in protest. He called a technical. I couldn't believe it! Jumping up to set the record straight, I caught my jacket on the hooks at the scorer's table used to display the signs announcing the number of fouls. I finally had to take my jacket off to get untangled. Gene Shue, then the coach of the Bullets, told me that they had filmed the whole episode. The players would run it again and again in the locker room; the Bullets liked seeing it so much that they included it in their film of the season's highlights. I'll disregard what that says about the Bullets' season.

The best officiating is anonymous; the referees control the game but don't intrude on the action. Personal clashes between the referees and players or coaches don't have a place in the game. Everyone appreciates the difficulty of the official's job, and though the officiating in the NBA now is better than it once was, there is still room for improvement. I think the League should consider adding to the number of officials who work a game. Two referees can't keep track of everything that happens. Other professional sports have increased the number of officials in order to keep pace with the bigger and faster athletes who are now playing. Basketball, I believe, would be wise to follow their example. The League is reluctant to change, however, because of the costs. Adding a third referee is no guarantee that the quality of officiating will improve, but I think it holds enough promise to be worth trying. If it were coupled with better training programs for young referees and a more rigorous selection process, I believe it would lead to a substantial upgrading for officiating.

Referees interested in working in the NBA now try out during the rookie camp each team holds in the summer. As many as 20 referees may try out during a single two-to-three day camp, officiating during scrimmages without any spectators around, for as few as ten minutes a day. That's just not enough time to observe them well. The League needs a training program, perhaps operated in conjunction with the NBA Officials' Association, to recruit and teach young officials. It's important for referees to start their training early, and to know the game well. They should be able to work their way up from high school to college ball, and then to the NBA. I think former players, particularly those who are just a step below the NBA players in their skills, would make the best referees. Not only would they know the game well, but they would have the speed and size to keep up with the players. The NBA now supervises the work of some officials in the Eastern Basketball League and the summer professional leagues, but it could be doing more. The NBA, as the highest level of basketball played, ought to have the best officiating. If the NBA owners will invest in programs to improve the training of referees, the game will get the officiating it deserves.

Management and the Draft

Running an NBA team is a business. Winning can be very profitable, but assembling a winning organization can also be costly. The best-managed basketball business, from a coach's point of view, is neither parsimonious nor meddling. It has to spend enough money to get good players and keep them happy, but it can't assume that writing the checks carries with it the right to intrude on the coach's job. The team owner, like the coach with his team, sets the tone of the business. In my experience, an owner who is not dependent on the revenue from the team is preferable to an owner who has to draw on the team's earnings. Building a winner can take a long time; an owner has to be able to sustain the team during lean stretches. The best owner is one who, having selected the people he wants to run the business, lets them do their jobs. He oversees but doesn't usurp the functions of the general manager, the director of player personnel and the coach. Nothing is more bothersome to a coach than an interfering owner.

The general manager of a team is responsible for its ordinary business operations. He negotiates and signs player contracts, arranges for the use of the arena and supervises the team's traveling schedule. On some teams he is also in charge of scouting and drafting, though most teams now—as does Portland—have a director of player personnel to scout and arrange player changes. The director of player personnel charts a team's future by the draft choices he makes. Beyond communicating my player needs to the director of player personnel, I have little to do with the draft. I expect the owner and general manager to let me do my job, and I assume the director of player personnel is capable of doing his.

When I was the general manager of the 76ers I was also in charge of the draft. At the time I joined the team, it had only one part-time scout. The owner resisted my requests for a full-time scout, though I should have fought him harder on it than I did. Now every team in the League has at least one full-time scout; in addition, a number of teams—including the Trail Blazers—subscribe to the services of Marty Blake and Associates, an independent scouting firm. Stu Inman, the Blazers' director of player personnel, is assisted by Bucky Buchwalter, a former coach, in preparing the list of players the Blazers hope to draft. And though they do an excellent job, like every NBA scout they've had to endure the frustration of some puzzling disappointments. Every NBA team has drafted players with "can't miss" labels who do, in fact, miss. A first round draft pick is always a player highly regarded by every scout and every team; the only surprises in the first round—or even in the first two rounds—are in the order in which players are picked, not in the players chosen. A team expected to take a big forward, for example, may take a ballhandling guard instead. But in both instances the players will be known to everyone involved in the draft. And yet in the last five years,

14 first round picks have failed to make it in the NBA. There's uncertainty in every draft. Portland's first round pick in 1977, for example, Rich Laurel, never did sign with the Blazers; after brief trials with two other teams, he was released from the League. On the other hand, T.R. Dunn, the Blazers' third pick, made the eleven-man roster. Lloyd Neal, who was also a third round pick, emerged as a fine NBA player; the two players chosen before him in 1973 are no longer playing. The roster of the Blazers 1976-77 championship team shows both sides of the draft; it had on it, along with six players taken in the first round, two second round picks, three third round choices, and one player who had not been drafted by any team.

The Blazers didn't sign Rich Laurel in 1977 because of excessive demands by his agent. I am not involved in the players' salary negotiations, nor would I want to be, but I am interested in seeing that players feel adequately compensated for the jobs they do. It is management's responsibility to assure that players are paid what they're worth. The salary structure on a team should be equitable; the best players should be paid the most, but no one should be paid excessively. Given today's salaries, it's sometimes hard to tell what is excessive. When I was coaching at Buffalo, Bob McAdoo, who was clearly the team's outstanding player, was paid less than Ernie DiGregorio, a flashy guard who had signed a very high salaried contract with the team's owner, Paul Snyder. When I decided that Ken Charles rather than DiGregorio deserved to start, McAdoo found an even stronger basis for his claim that he should be paid more than Ernie D. McAdoo wanted to renegotiate his contract. Synder did make an offer, but it was not one satisfactory to McAdoo. The consequence was that an initial inequity in the salaries paid to the Buffalo players affected the team's performance on the court.

A meddling management can affect a team in many ways, none of them good. The conflict over DiGregorio's salary at Buffalo was aggravated by Snyder's belief that my not starting

Ernie D was hurting the team at the gate. I was convinced, and the record of the team supported my view, that we were better off starting Charles. But Snyder never really thought so. A coach must have complete freedom to handle his players in the ways he thinks are best. If the owner doesn't like it, he can fire the coach. A coach who tolerates interference isn't doing his job anyway—whoever is doing the interfering has taken over the coach's role. I coached a player in Buffalo, whom we had acquired by trade, who told me that on his former team the owner had installed a telephone running from his private box high in the arena down to the bench. It was rumored that the owner would then send orders down to the coach telling him to make substitutions. I can't imagine a coach putting up with that. I also knew an owner who, because he was sure he knew what would attract fans to the arena, suggested strongly that his coach not start five black players. In addition to demeaning the coach and players, the idea was an insult to the integrity of the game. The coach, I am happy to say, ignored the suggestion.

The conflicts which sometimes arise between owners and coaches may be explained in part by the fact that they have certain qualities in common. Bruce Ogilvie, a psychologist interested in athletic motivation, studied the personalities of successful coaches and successful business executives, which most owners are. They shared, he discovered, three principal characteristics: a strong commitment to their jobs, often to the exclusion of other interests; transparent personalities, by which Oglivie meant that they made no effort to hide their true characters or their goals; and a powerful intellectual curiosity about their work, leading them on an endless search to find out everything they can about their jobs. People sharing these traits would obviously have trouble working together if they did not clearly delineate their roles. I believe the roles are clearly defined within the Trail Blazers' organization. I like the way the team is managed. The organization has abided by the agreement we made when I first took the job: they manage, I coach. That arrangement doesn't assure a winner, but it does mean that everyone will get a chance to do his job the best way he knows how. In the 1976-77 season, that accord worked out well.

PART III: THAT CHAMPIONSHIP SEASON

BUILDING THE BLAZERS

CHAPTER VI

WHEN I convened my first training camp as Trail Blazer coach in September, 1976, I was optimistic about the coming season. I knew we were a young team, but I also thought we had talent at every position. The player changes we had made over the summer added strength to the capable nucleus of players remaining on the team from the year before. My conversations with the players during the summer had persuaded me of their desire to play the style I intended to coach. The team as a whole had speed, quickness, and a positive attitude. I knew they were preparing to arrive at our training camp in good condition, ready to run the Ramsay mile and meet the rope jumping requirement. As the opening of training camp approached, I could hardly restrain my enthusiasm to get underway. As it turned out, I had to wait a little bit longer than I expected.

Training camp was scheduled to open with a team meeting at 7:00 p.m. at the motel where we were staying. I wanted to begin by laying down the ground rules for the team. Printed booklets detailing procedures for the team's conduct, including such matters as a dress code, the rules for players out with injuries, and a system of fines for missing or coming late to practice or meetings, were ready to distribute. We were ready to launch our championship season, but something was still missing. Three players hadn't yet arrived. Bill Walton strolled in at 7:04, Herm Gilliam and Maurice Lucas five minutes later. When everyone was finally settled, the team's trainer, Ron Culp, passed out the booklets. I announced matter-of-factly that there was a $2.00 per minute fine for anyone late to a meeting. "That's $8.00 for you, Bill, and $18.00 apiece for Herm and Luke."

It may not have seemed like the best way to begin a season, but the effect of this episode was actually beneficial. It taught two lessons better than my simply stating them ever could have: that I expected punctuality from each player, and that no one was immune from the team's rules. The team unity so notable in the Trail Blazers' play that season was engendered at that first team meeting.

The training camp went well from the first day. The turnout offense was easy to teach to players who wanted and were able to pass the ball. The team's ability to play tough, aggressive defense was quickly evident. Nothing happened to abate my enthusiasm, not even the occasional displays of sloppy basketball that the tedium and exhaustion of a rigorous training camp invariably produce. We were practicing twice a day in two-hour sessions, at ten in the morning and at five in the afternoon. We also met each evening to review the day's work and prepare for the next day's activities. The team sometimes played with flashes of brilliance, belying the brief association the players had had with one another. After one particularly sharp scrimmage, I called the players together. "We can win playing this way," I told them. "If we can play that tough, overplaying defense, with the strong rebounding and outlet passing, if we can push the ball up the floor when the fast-break is there, if we can get the kind of ball movement we've had today, we can win in this league." I could feel among the players an unspoken agreement with what I had said as they left the floor that day. Before playing a single game together, they were beginning to build confidence in themselves and their style of play. Not every practice, however, was as encouraging.

The next day, the team's play was as inept as it had been splendid the day before. Our scrimmage was marked by turnovers and loose defensive play, by poor passes and lackluster execution. Even in a team so young and recently formed, the play was inexcusably bad. I again called them together, contrasting the previous day's excellent play with the performance I had just observed. "We can win playing like we did yesterday," I reminded them, "but not if we play this way." The players knew the difference, as they were soon to prove.

By the time training camp ended, I thought the team had come together well. There had been a few surprises, but nothing discouraging. Dave Twardzik's play was superior to what I had expected, leading me to an adjustment in my plans for a starting lineup. I had initially considered using Hollins and Gilliam in the backcourt, with Davis and Twardzik as substitutes, but the combination of Twardzik's excellent play and a weakness in the ballhandling ability of a Hollins-Gilliam lineup persuaded me to start Dave along with Lionel. I didn't really appreciate Twardzik's overall skills until after training camp was underway. Despite Stu Inman's assurances to the contrary, I wasn't sure Dave was good enough to play very much for us. He doesn't look much like an NBA player. He's not very big, he doesn't have the speed of someone like Hollins or Davis, and he can't really jump that high. All he does is whatever he has to for the team to win. We were all astonished in training camp by Dave's ability to shoot a layup over the biggest players on the floor. He has a great first step to the basket and amazing control of his body in the air. After a few days of swatting vainly at Twardzik's spinning shots off the backboard, Walton was reduced to laughter at his inability to block Dave's shot. "Fudd," he'd exclaim, "you're great!"

Other than starting Twardzik, the team came together about as I had planned. Walton, of course, would play in the middle, with Robin Jones as his principal back-up. Maurice Lucas would start at big forward, though I had not really decided between him and Lloyd Neal before training camp began. Lloyd, however, was hampered by a knee injury which would require surgery before the end of the exhibition season. Luke established himself as the team's strongest big forward, though my plans to use him as a back-up center as well as a starting forward didn't prove out as well. Bob Gross would start at small forward, a position in the running game for which he was ideally suited. All of the players, from the regulars to the bench players, were ready to play as training camp ended. I was pleased with what we had accomplished in our first few weeks together.

As we were driving back to Portland at the conclusion of our fall camp, I told Jack McKinney, "We're going to win. I can feel it." Jack had the same positive feeling. The team had skill, it was unselfish, it was eager to play. When I told Jack I thought we could win, though, I didn't mean that I was sure we would be the next NBA champion. I did think, however, that we could win more than half our games and, by doing so, make the playoffs. We were too young, I felt, and too inexperienced to expect of ourselves anything so grandiose as a championship. We needed to take first things first. Portland had never had a winning season, let alone a trip to the playoffs, so achieving those two goals gave us plenty of incentive. I thought we could take that first step toward an eventual championship. Once we were in the playoffs, we could begin to think about winning it all. But first we had to get there.

Our play over the eight-game exhibition season sustained my hopes for a winning season, despite our slow start. In our first preseason home game against the Lakers, we were playing poorly. The players were too tight and anxious, not moving easily. The fans had yet to see in the team what I had seen so well in practice. During a lull in the action, I heard a voice call out from the stands. "Where are you going to be next year, Ramsay?" We went on to win that game, despite the grim reminder that in NBA coaching it's only the results that count. Before too long, all the criticism built up during six years of frustration over the Blazers' inability to win disappeared in the joyous celebration of the championship season.

We finished the exhibition season strongly with a win over Seattle. Our preseason record was five wins, three losses. At times we had played very well, but not yet with the overall consistency I expected to achieve. The quality of our play may have surprised some of our early season opponents. The Trail Blazers were certainly not very well known. Before a game with the Pistons in late October the broadcaster Jerry Gross, who was preparing profiles on each team, interviewed me. He was going to show each team in action, with a voice-over by its coach evaluating the team's players. When Jerry asked me who my starters were, I told him that Walton was the center, Lucas and Gross the forwards, and Hollins and Twardzik the guards. He gave me a puzzled look. "I know Bill," he said, "but Twardzik, Lucas?" He expected some elaboration.

"Jerry," I responded, "they are two good players, but you just haven't seen them because they've been playing in the ABA."

Hollins and Gross had played well as rookies, but no one in the media expected them to start on a team contending for a championship. I saw Jerry again after the game. We had beaten the Pistons 131 to 97, playing the way I knew we could. Jerry looked at me with real respect in his eyes. "Those guys can play. They really can play." Yes, I thought, they really can.

If any doubts about this team's ability remained, they were soon erased in one of the greatest performances I have ever seen. Early in November, the Philadelphia 76ers brought what everyone was calling the "wonder team" to Portland for a game against the Blazers. George McGinnis, Julius Erving, Doug Collins and company were the most celebrated team in the NBA, a nearly unanimous choice among journalists to win the League championship. The night before we were to play them, I went to Oakland to scout them in a game against the Warriors. They were indeed impressive in beating Golden State, but I thought them far from invincible. When I met the Blazers the next morning for our game day workout, I told them I was confident we could exploit a number of weaknesses in the 76ers' game. "We can run on this team," I said. "They're slow getting back on defense and our passing game should go great. They try to switch on every screen, which means that Bill ought to be able to hit the screener going to the basket on our post play with regularity." I had also noticed that in their zeal to score the Sixers often left the backcourt open, a situation made to order for our fastbreak. Given what happened, I think it is fair to say that my confidence was both well-founded and infectious.

As I came out on the court that night, I looked down to the end of the court where the 76ers were nonchalantly cruising through their warm-up. It was obvious that they expected an easy game. I thought to myself as I went to our bench, "They're not ready for us." Indeed they were not. We started the game in spectacular fashion, going ahead first nine to nothing, then twenty to four, then 36 to 16. The Sixers never recovered, and the Blazers never diminished the pace. The final score was 146-104 as the Unknowns soundly walloped the Superstars. It was a great win for everyone involved. In the fourth quarter, as he rested on the bench while his teammates finished the rout, Bill Walton received a remarkable spontaneous tribute from the Portland fans. When the scoreboard flashed the announcement that it was Bill's birthday, the audience rose as one to sing "Happy Birthday." Rather than detracting from the team's outstanding effort, that celebration recognized Walton's unique contribution to his team.

As I left the Coliseum that night in the cool November evening, I felt a deep sense of satisfaction. "We could have beaten any team in the world tonight," I thought to myself. "I coach a team that could beat any team in the world." It was a wonderful feeling. One game, however, does not make a season. I couldn't allow myself to savor the pleasures of the game for too long without losing track of what we still had to do. The biggest problem I had to deal with was our Jekyll and Hyde syndrome: we were good at home, but awful on the road.

We lost our first six games on the road. As well as we played at home, we played equally poorly on the road. During our long, early season dry spell in away games, we won twelve consecutive home games. The Trail Blazers over the years had built a well-deserved reputation as a poor road team, creating a psychological hurdle which we were having difficulty overcoming. We played without concentration or poise. Watching

Jekyll play one night and Hyde the next was a puzzling and frustrating experience.

I had known from the beginning of the season that coaching the young and inexperienced Trail Blazers would require patience and forbearance. I knew all along that we would make mistakes. But the contrast between our excellent play at home and our futility on the road was too vast to tolerate. I was sure we could win anywhere if we played our game. Stu Inman cautioned me against being too demanding. "I think you're putting incredible pressure on yourself," Stu told me. "You're expecting too much." Stu may have been correct, but I couldn't change what I am. I saw the potential in my team and wanted to see it realized. Nothing less than the best the Trail Blazers could give was acceptable to me. When their best effort was not forthcoming, I finally reached my limit.

I abandoned my policy of low-keyed patience after a loss to the Milwaukee Bucks, a team which had then lost nine straight games. We played like a high school team in a 115 to 106 loss, reaching the nadir of an already barren sojourn. We just could not win on the road. I was furious. After the game, as the players sat in the locker room contemplating the mysteries of their suddenly interesting shoelaces, I assailed them with an emotional critique of their ineffectual play. I would no longer tolerate a shoddy performance. I wanted results. I didn't want excuses. If we could beat the best teams in the League at home, we ought to be able to beat most teams on the road as well. In no uncertain terms I made it clear what I expected, banging the chalkboard with my fist for emphasis. I was unrelenting. My tirade concluded, I stalked out of the locker room to talk to the members of the press, still as hot with anger as I had been when the game ended.

I'm never very good at interviews on such occasions. Every question I was asked that night got a terse, one-line answer. The session didn't last long. It was clear to everyone present that I didn't feel much like talking. As the press conference ended, I returned to the locker room, tossed my coat over my arm, and set out on the long tramp back to the hotel, forswearing the comforts of the team bus. It was a frigid Milwaukee night, the temperature no more than ten degrees. In my mood, though, I was oblivious to the cold. When I got to the hotel lobby, I discovered that I was still carrying my coat. I think I could have walked all the way to Indianapolis, where we were scheduled to play the next night, with nothing but my wrath to keep me warm.

Our long drought finally ended with a close win over the Indiana Pacers. We still weren't playing as well as we could, but we had at least passed a crucial psychological barrier. In our next game, against Phoenix, we finally played with poise, confidence and aggressiveness against an opponent on its home floor. The win felt good. I told the players after the game how pleased I was with their performance, praising them now as earnestly as I had criticized them for their poor game in Milwaukee. We were beginning to solidify as a team, pulling together through the tough spots and mutally enjoying the pleasure of a difficult win. The team which I had imagined before training camp was slowly beginning to materialize. It didn't happen without some difficulty, however. Learning to win on the road helped the team coalesce, but the willingness of every player to accept his role on the team helped even more.

A potentially disruptive episode involving Maurice Lucas in an early season game against Atlanta demonstrated well the depth with which the team spirit was taking hold on the Trail Blazers. We were in a zone press against the Hawks after scoring a free throw. Maurice was out of position, a lapse I tried to remedy by signaling frantically to him to regain his proper floor position. He brushed aside my instructions with a "Don't bother me" gesture. I quickly called on Corky Calhoun to replace Maurice. Luke came out of the game angry. When Jack McKinney approached Maurice in order to explain the defensive adjustment we needed to make, Luke refused to talk to him. The situation had reached a critical point; I motioned for Lucas to come to me. I then did something I rarely do. Turning my back on the game in progress, I gave my full attention to Luke. "When I first met you this summer," I reminded him, "you asked that I treat you with respect. You said that I was the boss and you would do whatever I asked as long as I treated you like a man. I've done that. Don't get pissed off at me, I'm just trying to do whatever I have to do to win this game. Now get yourself together and I'll get you back in the game."

I soon called for Luke to re-enter the game, during the remainder of which he played well. We won going away. In the dressing room immediately afterwards, as is my custom, I called for the team's attention to begin my post-game evaluation. Before I could say a word, however, Luke stood up to say, "I want to apologize to Coach McKinney. I was out of order." Maurice showed real strength of character in that incident. He clearly established himself as a team man, acknowledging before his teammates and coaches that he had stepped out of bounds. It reaffirmed my position as the decision maker on the team, while firmly establishing the significance of Coach McKinney's role. A potentially ugly emotional event was transformed into a positive contribution to the team's unity.

We continued to work hard in practice, keeping our sights set on our season goals of a winning record and a place in the playoffs. We beat both the Knicks and the Celtics on the road, something no Blazer team had ever been able to do. Playing with consistency on the road was still a problem for us, but the team's confidence was growing. Bill Walton, apparently free at last from the nagging injuries that seemed always to strike him, was beginning to play as I knew he could. In a game at Chicago in late December, Bill put on a clinic. The game was close halfway through the third period. A Portland player was at the foul line, so Bill was back near our bench on the defensive end of the floor guarding against a Chicago fastbreak off a missed free throw. Bill said as he came over to me, "I'm hot as hell, but I can't get the ball." I told him, "Don't worry, I'll get the ball to you." We started running plays designed to free Bill, who was as hot as he claimed. He scored field goal after field goal over Chicago's center, Artis Gilmore. When the game ended, Bill had scored 29 points in a Blazer win. In his elation, Bill grabbed the game ball and hurled it high up into the stands. The Blazers were billed for the ball, but we were happy to pay. Walton was healthy, and we were winning some on the road. Our toughest tests, however, still lay ahead.

In mid-January we faced perhaps our hardest road trip—eight games in twelve days. I wanted at least a split on the trip. "Somehow," I thought to myself, "we've got to win at least four of these games." Not only was the schedule difficult, but we were without Lionel Hollins for five of the games. Lionel had been playing well, demonstrating around the league his exceptional defensive skills and marvelous speed, but suffered a depressed fracture from an elbow to the forehead in a game against the New Orleans Jazz. Our job would be more difficult without him.

We started off with a win over the Celtics, but then lost to the Bullets and the Hawks. We rebounded for wins over the Nets and the Cleveland Cavaliers, moving on to Houston for a game with the Rockets that ended in terrible disappointment. After leading by 19 points at halftime, we played poorly in the second half, losing a game we should have won. It was clear the next afternoon as we lost in San Antonio that we hadn't been able to shrug off the loss to Houston, though we didn't play all that poorly. We were now at three wins and four losses for the trip, with a tough game against Denver left to play. Our chances for a split seemed slight; Denver rarely lost at home. We would have to play well, but for the first half it didn't look like we were going to make it.

Denver was as good in the early part of the game as I had expected them to be, pulling out to a 19-point lead. We were hanging on, however, and closed the gap before the half ended. In the second half, we played some super basketball, defending strongly and running our offense with patience and poise. Having managed to hang in until the game was finally within our reach, we won it at the end with clutch plays. At the game's conclusion I raced onto the court with my arms upraised in a victory sign. I grabbed Bill Walton's hand in congratulations. The locker room was exuberant. We had accomplished what I had hoped we would on the long road trip.

After the game, Jack McKinney and I went out in the cold Denver night looking for a place to eat. "Jack," I remarked, "I think we've turned the corner. I think we've proven to ourselves that we can win on the road." We ended up at a spaghetti and pizza place feasting on spinach salad, joined by several other members of the Blazer entourage. The next day we learned that our victory at Denver had been earned at considerable cost.

Bill awakened the next morning to discover some soreness in his Achilles tendon, but couldn't point to anything specific in the Denver game which could account for the injury. He might have been kicked, or he may simply have strained it. Though he did play in our next home game, the tendon was too painful for him to be effective. Walton missed the next ten games, joining Lloyd Neal on the injury list. The Denver game had demonstrated our ability to win big games on the road, but the period that followed showed just as clearly how crucial Bill Walton was in any plans we had for a successful season. With both Bill and Lloyd out with injuries, Robin Jones had to play long minutes, while Lucas had to play even longer minutes at both center and big forward. Corky Calhoun moved into Lloyd's spot as the back-up at big forward. Luke played great basketball, exhausting himself game after game in an effort to keep up the Blazers' winning ways. The team showed great courage in contesting every game down to the closing minutes, playing hard in defeat. Handicapped by injuries, the team simply wore down in the late stages of a game, losing all but two games during Bill's absence. Our playoff hopes were still alive, but the team's confidence was sagging.

Sustaining the team's spirit through the low points of the season was my job. I gave the players constant encouragement, praising them for their hard work in practice and their unflagging effort in our long, depressing string of losing causes. I was proud of them for not giving up on themselves, as I frequently told them. The effort was always there, even as we lost. Staying with our game plan, even if Robin Jones could not make the back door pass the way Bill could, or if Corky couldn't play at big forward like Lloyd was able to, was crucial to our team's eventual success. We were overmatched, but never outfought. Defeat, though it is never tolerable, was easier to accept under the circumstances we were then facing. I knew that if we could just hang on, playing our game as best we could, we would be able to renew our drive to the playoffs once the injured players rejoined us.

I greeted Walton's return to the line-up in February with a great sense of relief. Every player could now expect a greater return for his effort. Our turnabout was immediate. In Bill's first game back, we had a big homecourt win over Boston. The game was close, with Bill only able to play for twenty minutes, but his presence gave us a great psychological lift. I thought we were on our way to good things again, but my optimism was premature. In a game in early March against the Sixers, in which Bill got overtired from playing too long after his layoff, he sprained his ankle by coming down off-balance with a rebound. I blamed myself for not resting him more, knowing that fatigue made him susceptible to injury. Bill missed the next five games, four of which we lost. Would we ever be healthy?

Our final drive for a playoff berth began with the return of Bill and Lloyd to the roster in mid-March. Lionel Hollins had recovered from his skull injury as well. We finished the season strongly, holding off a strong challenge from the Warriors for our playoff spot. The key game of that period took place in Oakland on March 17, a game we had to win in order to stay in second place. We had a great game, with Walton playing magnificently. Larry Steele also had one of the finest games of his career, scoring 27 points to go along with his nine rebounds and six assists. Because of the injuries Lionel and Dave Twardzik had suffered during the season, Steele had been playing at a guard position more than I had expected to use him there. His ability to come off the bench as either a small forward or a guard was invaluable to the team, but his guard play in particular had been so outstanding that I kept him in the guard rotation after Dave and Lionel had recovered. Doing so moved Herm Gilliam down to the fifth guard's spot, a role he was not happy to assume.

I talked with Herm at length about his place on the team, impressing upon him the possibility that he might work his way back into the third guard's spot. Gilliam continued to work hard in practice, making probably the most difficult adjustment of any player to the style of play we were using. Later in the season we had an opportunity to trade Herm to New Orleans, where he would play more but for a team less likely to make the playoffs. Before making any deal, though, I talked with him about it. I made it clear that I wanted him on the team, that I thought his experience would be valuable to us in the playoffs, but that the choice was his to make. After consulting with his wife and deliberating for awhile, Herm told me that he preferred to stay with the Blazers. It was an important decision for the Blazers. Gilliam did, in fact, have some exceptional moments for us in the playoffs.

On April 1, 1977, the Portland Trail Blazers clinched a playoff position for the first time in the team's history by defeating the Warriors in Portland. No April fool—we had done it. Our goal of reaching the playoffs had been realized. As I walked off the floor after the game, I noticed the message board above me flashing "Playoffs! Playoffs!" "OK," I thought to myself, "you've reached the first plateau. Now let's see if you can get the big one." For the first time all season, I let myself think about winning the championship. We had a shot at it now. In the locker room after the game I congratulated the players, sharing with them the ambition I now allowed myself to hold. "We can do it," I assured them. "We know we can beat anybody. We have to play our game well to do it, but we have a great chance. Let's make the most of it."

During the remainder of the regular season, we worked to prepare ourselves for the playoffs. I wanted everyone rested and at his physical peak. I used the same rotation in games that

I intended to use in the playoffs, reemphasizing the roles of each player. We ran drills in practice to sharpen individual skills and bring our team game into the playoffs at its peak. Our goal now was nothing less than winning the NBA Championship. Chicago, we learned, would be our first opponent in the playoffs.

WINNING THE CHAMPIONSHIP

CHAPTER VII

THE Bulls finished their season with a flourish, compiling the best record in the league over the last two months after a sluggish start. We knew they would be tough, but for the only time in the playoffs we had the home court advantage. As events were to prove, it was an edge we surely needed. We split the first two games, in each of which the home team won, setting up the rubber match in Portland. Each game was a hard fought, well played contest. The third game was close in the final seconds, the Blazers leading 100 to 98. With only 15 seconds remaining, the key play of the series—and the most significant shot of the season—was made by Lionel Hollins. As the twenty-four second clock expired, Lionel drilled a jumper from the top of the circle, clinching our victory. The final score was 106 to 98, the final four points coming off free throws as Chicago fouled in its desperate attempts to get the ball. We had made it through the first round.

The series with the Bulls could hardly have been tougher. Hard, physical play marked each game; in the third game, in fact, three Blazers had fouled out. Hollins had not been shooting well in the final game, though he was true when it counted. After the game, Herm Gilliam came up to me with a big grin on his face. "Coach," he asked, "how come you picked Lionel to take that shot? He was only four for fifteen!" It wasn't that tough a decision, actually, since Luças, Walton and Twardzik were the Blazers who had fouled out.

"Herm," I replied, "I knew he was going to make it." Herm could only shake his head and laugh, wondering at my clairvoyance. I did think Lionel was the best player to have shoot, in spite of his earlier difficulties getting the ball to go down. Lionel was my man and he didn't fail me.

Our next opponent was Denver, which had the advantage of playing the first two games on its home court. The key play in the Denver series, unlike the one against Chicago, came early—it occurred, in fact, late in the first game. We trailed by a single point with 20 seconds left to play. During a timeout we called, I set up a play for us to run that called for a pass from Lucas to Gross at the top of the circle, followed by a backdoor play for Twardzik going to the basket. Denver had been overplaying on the weak side pass, a defensive strategy. that I was certain would give Dave an opportunity to get free for a layup. But a funny thing happened on the way to the execution of that play. When Lucas got the ball, he didn't pass to Gross. Instead, he backed his man into the lane and shot a turn-around jumper over him right off the backboard and into the basket. Denver got the ball back, trailing by one point with eleven seconds to play. They wanted to get the ball to David Thompson, but we overplayed the pass. Unable to make the play he wanted, Ted McLain was forced to take a bad shot that missed as time ran out. We had overcome Denver's home court advantage.

Pandemonium in the locker room! The players pounced on Luke, punching him in glee, ruffling his neatly trimmed hair, laughing ecstatically. Walton's shouted epithet perfectly summarized what everyone felt: "Now that's some shit!" I was elated, hugging Jack McKinney in celebration. Even Ron Culp, our unflappable trainer, joined in the cheering. As the din subsided, I called for everyone's attention. Looking sternly in Lucas' direction, I announced in as solemn a voice as I could manage, "Luke, you're fined fifty dollars for not running the play." But the joke was too obvious, and I couldn't keep from grinning. The celebration resumed. It was a great night, giving promise of victories to come. We defeated Denver in the second round of the playoffs, four games to two. Dave Twardzik severely sprained his ankle in the fifth game, but even the loss of a fine player like Dave didn't stall our drive to the championship.

Our next opponent was the Los Angeles Lakers, a team which had given us more than we could handle in our first three games against them during the regular season. In our last home game of the season we had beaten the Lakers 145-116, but I didn't expect any easy wins in the playoff series. The Lakers, with the best record in the league, had also earned the home court advantage. But while we had defeated Denver in six games, the Lakers were caught in a seven game struggle against the Warriors. Jack McKinney and I went to Los Angeles to watch the final game of the series. It was a profitable trip.

The Warriors used an effective defensive strategy against the Lakers, opening up an early ten-point lead. The Warrior guards forced the Laker guards to bring the ball up the right side of the court, denying them the opportunity to make an easy pass to Abdul-Jabbar in his favorite spot on the left side of the floor. When Kareem gets the ball in his hooking station, he is nearly unstoppable on a rolling move across the lane. Making it difficult for Kareem to get the ball where he wanted it was an effective idea, though the Warriors were not altogether successful in executing it. The Lakers eventually won the game, but I had learned a valuable lesson from the team they beat. Our adaptation of the Warriors' defensive plan helped us win against the Lakers.

The first two games against the Lakers were in Los Angeles. In the opening game of the series, the Blazers played just as I imagined they could at their best. Our great running, excellent timing and superb passing enabled us to open up a 61-43 lead at halftime. We had been able to force the Laker guards out of their game by picking them up in the backcourt and forcing them to the right side. The Lakers, who had set an NBA record by winning 37 games at home while losing only four, seemed stunned by what was happening. They didn't expect to lose on their floor, but we beat them 121 to 109. In the second game, however, the Lakers were clearly determined to resume their winning ways at home.

Using a tough, physically aggressive defense, the Lakers shut down our cutting game in our second meeting. Because of their strong defense, we weren't able to execute our offense well. We couldn't move the ball the way we had in the first game, nor did we have speed and quickness in our running game. The Lakers were jamming the lane to prevent us from penetrating and passing in close to the basket, challenging us to score from the perimeter. We needed someone to make some baskets from outside to relieve the pressure in the lane. Herm Gilliam, whom I had urged to stay with the Blazers for precisely this reason, came off the bench to give us a great game. He and Hollins were both superb, but Herm's hot hand finally won for us. Lionel's eight steals and Gilliam's 24 points, fourteen of which came in the final period, enabled us to win an extremely difficult game on the road. We returned to Portland leading in the series two games to none.

The two remaining games in Portland were as demanding as the second game in Los Angeles had been. Bill Walton played superbly, making clutch field goals and defending strongly against Abdul-Jabbar. Bill's overall team play was outstanding as well, marked by excellent rebounding and great passing. John Davis also played well in our four straight wins over the Lakers. That John played well was not surprising to me, but I suspect that the Lakers, who had chosen Earl Tatum ahead of Davis in the draft, didn't realize the full extent of John's skills.

After Dave Twardzik injured his ankle, John moved into the starting lineup. I knew he was ready to play, but I was leaning toward Larry Steele as Dave's replacement, figuring that Larry's experience would hold us in good stead in the pressures of a playoff series. As I deliberated, I recalled John's having approached me before the Chicago series one day after practice. "Coach, I'm not complaining," he had said to me then in his modest way, "but I think I can help." Despite his diffident manner, John was not lacking in self-confidence. I had told him then, "Okay, John, when the time is right, I'll have a use for you." I wondered now if the time had not come. I consulted with Walton and McKinney. When I asked Bill whom he thought we should use, his reply was immediate. "Johnny Davis," he said. "We can run with Johnny." McKinney concurred. I accepted their judgement, which proved itself sound. John was not only great in the final game against the Nuggets, scoring 25 points, but he played with a veteran's poise in the series against the Lakers.

Because Houston and Philadelphia were still playing for the Eastern Conference Championship, we had a nine-day wait between the final game of our sweep over the Lakers and the beginning of the NBA Championship series. We worked hard in practice, but lost the sharpness in our execution which only competition can provide. Philadelphia, our eventual opponent, had not only the home court advantage but also the edge of having played more recently. We were ragged but tough in the first game, losing 107 to 101. Julius Erving and Doug Collins both played well against us, together scoring more than sixty of their team's points. In the second game, however, we were only ragged. The Sixers ran right past us, taking advantage of the 29 turnovers we committed. In the final minutes of the game, Bob Gross was thrown to the floor by Darrell Dawkins. The Sixers' young center swung Bobby down in an attempt to wrest the ball from him after they had both grabbed it off the backboard. When Bob voiced his objections, Dawkins took a swing at him. The punch missed Gross, instead catching Doug Collins above his right eye. But the trouble was just beginning.

I had sensed the danger as soon as Dawkins and Gross began to struggle for the ball. I started to move from my position on the sideline to get between the two players, but to my astonishment was stopped by referee Richie Powers. Putting both his hands on my chest, he pushed me back toward the sidelines. "You get off the floor," he said repeatedly. I had no alternative but to comply. But while Powers was herding me toward the bench, Maurice Lucas rushed toward Dawkins and punched him in the side of the head. The two then squared off, though no more blows were landed. I raced onto the floor, stepping between Luke and Dawkins. Running straight toward

Dawkins, I shouted, "Get out of here! Get out of here!" Fans who had broken from the stands began to appear on the floor. It seemed, for a brief moment, that the whole Spectrum was going to erupt. I stayed at midcourt, glaring at Dawkins, who seemed puzzled by my presence there. I heard someone from the Philadelphia bench say, "Take it easy, Jack." Holding my ground between Dawkins and Lucas, I yelled back in the direction of whomever was urging caution on me. "Bullshit," I hollered, in no mood to debate. As I remained at center court, order was slowly restored. Luke and Dawkins were both ejected, and the game ground on to its miserable conclusion. We lost big, 107 to 89.

Tensions were still high after the game. My wife, Jean, two of my daughters and their husbands, and my son, John, were all at the game. They waited afterwards to accompany me to the hotel. A couple of Philadelphia fans wanted to continue the action in the parking lot. I was still hot, but didn't want to give them the satisfaction of seeing my anger. Cautioning my son and sons-in-law to ignore the taunts and insults, I left the parking lot for the trip back to the hotel.

Most of that night was spent reflecting on our two opening losses to Philadelphia. I still had confidence in my team, but I knew we weren't playing up to our ability. The lay-off had hurt, and the pressures of a championship series were evident. Lucas and Hollins were clearly tight, while John Davis showed signs for the first time in the playoffs that he was feeling the pressure. Mulling over what had happened, I found nothing to dissuade me from my initial optimism. We were a young team, susceptible to a little nervousness in the early going of an important series, but we were also very good. We still had a chance to prove it. As the first signs of the grey dawn intruded on my meditation, I realized that I was confident and relaxed. I hadn't slept at all, and we were still down two games to none against the Sixers, but I was sure we were heading back to better things in Portland.

On the plane home the next day, McKinney and I talked about the possibility of restoring Dave Twardzik to the starting lineup. Jack suggested that Dave might supply the poise we had been missing in the first two games. I had given the same idea some thought the night before, but had rejected it in favor of the notion that we simply had to get back to playing the way we wanted to play. If we played the Sixers the way we had played the Nuggets and the Lakers, we would do equally well. If, on the other hand, I started making changes in the lineup, it would tell the players that I had lost confidence in their ability to play our game. And, in fact, I had not lost confidence. I wanted the players to believe, as I did, that our best effort would produce victories, that we could win with the players we had been winning with before. The starting lineup remained as it had been. In discussing all of this with the players upon our return, I found them in agreement with me. We would just have to play better basketball.

In the third game we began the return to what we did best. Lucas helped set the mood when, as the starting lineups were introduced, he ran down to the Sixers' bench to shake hands with Darrell Dawkins and wish him luck. It was a fine gesture. Then, back before the home folks, we started again to play the basketball they were accustomed to seeing. The third game ended with the Blazers on top, 129-107. We were even better in the fourth game, finally playing the way I knew we could. I sensed an ebbing in the Sixers' confidence, but we still had to beat them on the road. Carrying with us the momentum of the third and fourth games, we beat Philadelphia in the fifth game at the Spectrum. Now we had to win one more at home.

The final game of the championship series was a great one. Though we built up a twelve-point halftime lead, the Sixers fought back to within two points as the game wound to its conclusion. The defense was ferocious in the closing seconds. Finally, with but five seconds remaining, Philadelphia had a final chance to tie the game in regulation time. George

McGinnis worked free for a short jump shot, but it bounced wide off the rim. Bill Walton tapped the ball toward the backcourt, where it was retrieved by John Davis as the clock ran out. We had done it! We had won the playoffs. Given the opportunity, we had seized it. I was overjoyed.

In the bedlam of the locker room after our victory, John Davis clasped my hand, looked at me with those soft brown eyes and said, "Coach, I want to thank you for having the confidence in me to leave me in there at the end of the game."

"John, you were doing the job," I replied. "I always go with the players who are doing the job." I was so pleased to hear him say that, though. Even amidst the larger satisfaction of winning the NBA Championship, the pleasure of hearing a player tell me how much what I had done mattered to him was a significant event. There are always small rewards on the road to larger dreams.

I was proud of what we had done. I had reached the goal I had been striving for through eleven years of college coaching and nine years in the NBA—a championship. I was, for now, the coach of the best basketball team in the world! And how I admired the players on that team; young and inexperienced, struggling with injuries, battling to keep their confidence, they had played with a selflessness and strength of purpose throughout the long season. They had played "our game" when it mattered, asserting themselves in the toughest competition. They—and I—were champions.

Leaving the tumult of the locker room, I joined family and friends for a short post-game celebration. Afterwards I wanted to be by myself for awhile. I drove to my home on a lake outside of Portland, got into my swimming trunks, dove into the lake and swam until my arms ached. Finally exhausted, I lay on my back and floated in the water, looked up into the bright blue Oregon sky, and felt utterly at peace with the world.